001.942
V182i

D1179999

001.942   Vallée
V182i   The invisible college

CHRISTIAN HERITAGE COLLEGE
2100 Greenfield Dr.
El Cajon, CA 92021

The
Invisible College

The
Invisible College

*What a Group of Scientists
Has Discovered About
UFO Influences
on the Human Race*

Jacques Vallee

E. P. DUTTON & CO., INC.
New York

To

Gerald Askevold

LIBRARY OF CONGRESS CATALOGING IN PUBLICATION DATA

Vallée, Jacques.
  The invisible college.

  Bibliography: p.
  Includes index.
  1. Flying saucers.   I. Title.
TL789.V336 1975   001.9'42   75-12843

Copyright © 1975 by Jacques Vallee
All rights reserved. Printed in the U.S.A.
First Edition

10 9 8 7 6 5 4 3 2

No part of this publication may be reproduced or transmitted in any form
or by any means, electronic or mechanical, including photocopy, recording, or any information storage and retrieval system now known or to be
invented, without permission in writing from the publisher, except by a
reviewer who wishes to quote brief passages in connection with a review
written for inclusion in a magazine, newspaper or broadcast.

Published simultaneously in Canada by Clarke, Irwin & Company
Limited, Toronto and Vancouver
ISBN: 0-525-13470-0

Contents

16519

Introduction

In the last twenty-five years, thousands of people have reported the persistent appearances of UFO phenomena. A careful examination of the patterns of these reports has already shown that they follow definite laws for which no explanation has been found. These statistical facts have been adequately documented elsewhere [1] and will not concern us here. Instead we will examine a more exciting subject: the role of this phenomenon and its impact on each of us. The aim of this book is to offer a new point of view on UFOs.

It has become important to pose the UFO "problem" in a new fashion because our cultural beliefs regarding the existence of forms of consciousness elsewhere in the universe are undergoing major shifts. Perhaps these shifts have been precipitated by the realization that outer space has been opened to man and by the feeling of the smallness and the isolation of our planet brought back by astronauts. Perhaps they are flowing from the hope that other civilizations may already have solved the economic and social problems that concern every country on earth today. The scope and impact of this cultural change have received some attention, but no attempt has yet been made to understand its basic mechanism.

In this book I propose to examine the hypothesis that

1. See in particular the book *Challenge to Science* by Jacques and Janine Vallee (Chicago: Regnery, 1966) and the paper "Basic Patterns in UFO Observations" by Claude Poher and Jacques Vallee, *Paper 75–42, the American Institute of Aeronautics and Astronautics* (January, 1975), 13th Aerospace Sciences Meeting.

UFOs may constitute a control system; that they are not necessarily caused by extraterrestrial visitors, nor the result of misidentifications and hoaxes on the part of deluded witnesses. If the hypothesis is true, then what the witnesses have seen were manifestations of a process not unlike that of a thermostat in a house. The thermostat is a mechanism that stabilizes the relationship between our body temperature requirements and the changing weather outside. Similarly, UFOs may serve to stabilize the relationship between man's consciousness needs and the evolving complexities of the world which he must understand. This book will explore this phenomenon.

Among those of my scientific colleagues who have taken an interest in UFOs, there have been two major approaches, which might be termed "technological" and "psychological." Several physicists and engineers have examined UFO reports from a "nuts and bolts" point of view; on the other hand, the same UFO reports have been interpreted by psychologists as archetypes or as the fulfillment of a psychological need of the percipient. Modern science developed on the premise that these two domains of the physical and the psychological must always be carefully separated. In my view this distinction, although convenient, has been arbitrary. The UFO phenomenon is a direct challenge to this arbitrary dichotomy between physical reality and spiritual reality.

In this book I will not confine myself to the examination of the physical reality, but will frankly step from this to the experiential and even to the mythical. I will approach this inquiry within the framework of *descriptive phenomenology,* which social scientist Cynthia Nelson has defined as follows:

> Descriptive phenomenology attempts to communicate the quality and structure of experiences, be they clear and symbolically defined . . . or diffuse and even not

symbolized. Its subject matter is any concrete phenomenon in experience.[2]

Instead of asking, like the physicist, "Does the phenomenon interact with measurable quantities of its environment?" or, like the psychologist, "What mental impulses or behavioral needs does the report fulfill?" we will review what is experienced by the witnesses; we will observe what they do as a result of these experiences; and we will attempt to correlate them within a total framework.

In 1968, during the months following the Six-Day War, many people claimed to have witnessed apparitions of the Virgin Mary in Zeitoun (Egypt). Cynthia Nelson was led to ask the question of the meaning of that reality in a way that is directly applicable to our study of UFOs:

> As phenomenologists we suspend judgment as to whether the apparition is *really real* (a question for scientific naturalism) and attempt rather to understand what people do when confronting stress. If men define situations as real they are real in their consequences.[3]

In this sense the UFO phenomenon is undoubtedly real. What does it mean, then, to say that it may represent a control system? And what is the quantity that is being controlled? I will try to show that what takes place through close encounters with UFOs is control of human beliefs, control of the relationship between our consciousness and physical reality, that this control has been in force throughout history, and that it is of secondary importance that it should now assume the form of sightings of space visitors.

When the object we call UFO is visible to us in the real-

2. From a paper, "Stress, Religious Experience and Mental Health: A Phenomenological View," presented at the Third International Congress of Social Psychiatry, Zagreb, 1970.
    3. *Ibid.*

ity of everyday life, I think that it constitutes *both* a physical entity with mass, inertia, volume, etc., which we can measure, *and* a window toward another mode of reality for at least some of the percipients. Is this why witnesses can give us at the same time a consistent narrative ("At 1:35 I was driving on highway 58 . . .") and a description of contact with forms of life that fit no acceptable framework? These forms of life may be similar to projections; they may be real, yet a product of our dreams. Like our dreams, we can look into their hidden meaning, or we can ignore them. But like our dreams, they may also shape what we think of as our lives in ways that we do not yet understand.

I might as well confess at the outset that I have seen phenomena I can only call UFOs. I have not only seen them, but on two occasions in the course of my professional work have tracked them, using small telescopes called theodolites. A few of my astronomer colleagues had made similar observations, and after making inquiries, we became aware of many similar sightings by professional astronomers the world over.

The objects we were tracking were not spectacular, but the reaction they elicited among French scientists at the time fascinated me. Instead of asking if these seemingly maneuverable and "impossible" objects could be a manifestation of some advanced technology (and in some cases it may well have been terrestrial), they thought only of suppressing their manifestation. They did this by denying every observation, by blaming it on airplanes when the documentation was unassailable, and by destroying the data when it was demonstrated to them that no airplane could have behaved as the objects did.

The insight I derived from this early experience with scientific skepticism proved invaluable. It brought me into contact with a number of scientists who, like myself, wanted to understand the nature of the UFO phenomenon, and were especially bent upon determining whether or not it had an intelligent origin. This group has grown larger over the years. Whimsically, it calls itself the "Invisible College."

Dr. J. Allen Hynek, in an article called "The UFO Mystery," published in the *FBI Bulletin* (Vol. 44, no. 2, Feb. 1975), has said:

> Way back in the "dark ages" of science, when scientists themselves were suspected of being in league with the Devil, they had to work privately. They often met clandestinely to exchange views and the results of their various experiments. For this reason, they called themselves the Invisible College. And it remained invisible until the scientists of that day gained respectability when the Royal Society was chartered by Charles II in the early 1660's.

My interest in UFOs has gone through several phases during this period, but my curiosity about the behavior of scientists who destroy, distort, or simply ignore the very facts they are supposed to investigate, has never been satisfied. Scientists are not the only ones to blame for the unfortunate stigma that is still attached to the subject of UFOs, but such a gap has appeared between their official beliefs and the beliefs of millions of people that a re-examination of the entire problem is now necessary.

We have, on one hand, the facts—thousands of unexplained observations by reliable witnesses. They stand as a monument to the limitations of our understanding. I will not enumerate these cases again. The curious reader will find them in such accessible places as the works of J. Allen Hynek, of Aimé Michel, John Fuller, and others (see the bibliography at the end of this book). One of my own earlier books, *Passport to Magonia*, contains a catalogue of 923 unexplained UFO landings, and the size of this evidence is increasing daily.

We have, on the other hand, a paucity of theories to account for this richness of data. Either this must be invention, delusion, hoax, and mirages, the experts tell us, or else we are being visited by an extraterrestrial race. I cannot subscribe to either explanation. I have argued for many years that the phenomenon could not be explained by hoax and illusion alone, that it contains an opportunity for genuinely new knowledge. In this book I hope to show why these unexplained observations need not represent a visitation from space visitors.

Much of my motivation for examining critically the extraterrestrial theory has come from a study of the information of witness accounts, which I processed on a computer using modern techniques of analysis. Many of these accounts describe the occupants of the craft; this material is rich enough for us to form a good idea of these beings' physiology and behavior, if it in fact corresponded to the conditions of biological evolution we can assume on other planets. What we obtain instead is a picture of a different level of existence, a reality that seems to cut through our own at right angles. It is what I call the reality of Magonia. But there is more.

No theory of UFOs can be deemed acceptable if it does not account for the reported psychic effects produced by these objects. By "psychic effects" I refer to the space-time distortions experienced by percipients of craft-like devices which appear or "fade away" on the spot, in ways that are reminiscent of descriptions of "materializations" in the spiritualist literature. The data also show that many witnesses have had unique experiences with apparently "alien" voices or thoughts in connection with the sightings. But I am especially referring to the fact that certain witnesses have been changed in a manner that is not explained by the events they claim to have observed. The best way to illustrate the complexity of these psychic effects is to examine two examples that are particularly instructive.

In October, 1973, I met a man who wanted to discuss with me what he called his "mission." He was a neatly dressed engineering executive who wore a dark suit and thick glasses. He stressed the importance of preserving his anonymity—he had experienced a great change in his life, he said, as a result of which he had come to the United States where he was now working with an electronic company. The change in his life had occurred when he had been taken aboard a flying saucer and had been taught "certain things." Contrary to most contactees, however, he sought no publicity, had no message to deliver to humanity, and did not claim to understand what had happened to him. He only knew that he was no longer the same person.

At the time of this encounter I had been for over a year in touch with another man whose story was similar but on the veracity of which I had reserved judgment. This other man was Uri Geller, the Israeli psychic who began an entertainment career as a stage magician but later puzzled the scientists who tested his abilities in the laboratory. Like the engineer, Geller had been inside what he described as a UFO. Like him, he had experienced a major life change and left his country. Like him, he felt that he had been given a "mission" and that he was the center of peculiar physical effects. So, when I met the engineer, instead of brushing aside the entire story—as I might have done before my acquaintance with Geller—I spent several hours listening to him with an open mind trying to understand his experiences and his motivations.

This series of events had begun in July, 1961, when the engineer, who was then a student, was walking through the countryside with four other men during an archeological field trip. At some point, he found himself separated from the group, wandered behind a cluster of trees, where suddenly he saw an object on the ground; it was a disk-shaped vehicle about twenty feet wide with a translucent "elevator" that lifted him to a cabin.

As in a dream or a movie, the vehicle transported him into a desolate area far away from this spot and landed near a large machine reminiscent of a computer, about five feet high and twenty feet long, with row after row of "recordings." It was not a teaching machine of any known earthly type: during the three hours he spent with the device his impression was that it kept playing these recordings and "feeding their contents directly into his brain." After this session he flew back alone. Eighteen days had elapsed as far as his friends and family were concerned. His father, a government official, had caused several police and military units to look for him. He was found within feet of the spot where he had last been seen. He still wore the same flower at his buttonhole. His clothes were impeccable. He did not need a shave.

The story was unbelievable, as the witness himself soon realized. To satisfy the unwanted curiosity of the numerous people who bothered his family, he "confessed" that it had been a joke. This explanation had the desired effect, and the case was gradually forgotten.

In the meantime this man's life was changing in several ways. For example, for the first six months after the incident, he required an abnormal amount of sleep; he would fall asleep about six in the evening and not wake up until seven in the morning. Then the pattern changed, and he required less and less sleep. Now he says that he requires only a few hours of sleep each night. And also, in the University courses he attended, everything that was taught now came to him with perfect clarity and total recall. Moreover, he stopped dreaming (or recalling his dreams). Finally, he states that he has not experienced sickness in any form since the incident.

This man's experiences following the UFO encounter are very similar to those of a number of individuals, only a few of whom attempt to publicize their observations.

Uri Geller is an example of one UFO "percipient" who developed some rather extraordinary beliefs about himself and about the future as a result of what he describes as an encounter with a flying saucer. An American parapsychologist, Dr. Andrija Puharich, brought Geller to the United States in 1971 and arranged for the young man to be studied under laboratory conditions at several scientific institutions. Geller's abilities include what can best be described as the triggering of a force which affects material objects, and which sometimes even seems to lead to dematerializations. Many of the manifestations around him are similar to classical "poltergeist" phenomena as described in the folklore of many countries: mysterious breakage and disappearance of objects, usually ascribed to the imagination of the witnesses. The puzzling fact here is that some phenomena affecting mass and inertia appear to be reproducible in the laboratory. Most remarkable for our purpose, however, is the fact that Geller believes himself invested with a mission, given to him by a mysterious space source. Some of his followers even suggest that he might be a Messiah.

The engineer whose experiences I am summarizing here has developed along lines similar to Geller, although his psychological makeup is considerably different. He is withdrawn and secretive, while Geller is a showman. The engineer is a very quiet and well-organized man whose greatest wish is to remain unknown. He feels that he has received certain information from the "teaching machine," that he has acquired the ability to "leave his body," that he is now able to transfer his consciousness at will into other objects or into space, and that he can trigger a psychokinetic power similar to that of Geller, who claims that he bends or breaks objects by pure thought.

The most directly verifiable consequence of this "incident" in the engineer's life has been his departure from his country to pursue his "mission" in the United States, more specifically in California. Here, he states, some major changes will take place. Although he feels *they will be social and political in nature,* he does not claim to have been given any particular message to announce to the world. The entire story is absurd, yet disturbing.

"Absurd," too, is the change in his eyesight caused by the experience. Prior to his alleged abduction this man had perfect eyesight in both eyes. It deteriorated rapidly afterward, a fact he attributes to a blinding, blinking light that was situated on top of the "machine." Some sort of vibration generated pain under the ear, at the base of the skull, throughout the experience. And a last absurd detail is this one: the witness states that he saw a vehicle and a machine—but he did not see a pilot, nor an occupant, nor any identifiable form of intelligent life in connection with these devices!

The common denominator in these two stories is the feeling of absurdity caused by the superimposition of psychic effects—psychokinesis, telepathy, travel to a different space-time frame—to the array of physical descriptions that have come to characterize the UFO phenomenon in general. Both these men claim to have observed a craft, to have entered it, and to have received information from visible and tangible devices. It is by concentrating upon the nature of this apparent absurdity that we can start looking for a general framework within which these experiences can find an interpretation.

Four major elements have combined in the last few years to shape a new framework for the study of UFO reports, a framework I will refer to in Chapter Five as "The Hilltop Theory." These four elements that forced a revision of previous ideas about UFOs (such as the "mass psychosis" idea and the "space visitors" idea) are: (1) the psychic component present in the apparent space and time alterations and in the information transfer reported by the percipients; (2) the nature of personal, social, and governmental reaction to the phenomenon, which can be described as triple coverup; (3) the observation of patterns of belief (akin to a new religious or mystical movement) among those who claim to be in contact with nonhuman intelligences; and (4) the sophisticated groups which are already exploiting these patterns, such as the UMMO organization in Spain. A chapter will be devoted to each one of the elements.

The new framework opens areas of investigation which have not until now been tied to the analysis of the total phenomenon, notably the investigation of the religious experience and the so-called "miracles," which we will introduce in Chapter Six, and the reports of psychic phenomena, such as those exhibited by Geller.

These are the points on which we will build a concept of the purpose of the technology that produces the modern signs in the sky—a technology that can assume many more surprising forms than it has so far shown.

Every human activity has a secret side. Science does not escape this rule. Beyond the dry, humorless reporting of experiments in the pages of technical magazines there is the reality of research as it is lived by many men and women. Much of their existence is spent gathering data and observing facts. *Not all the data they gather see the light of day. Not all the facts they observe become public knowledge.* As the "Century of Science" draws to an end, more and more of the material that researchers discover fails to be published because it fits into no convenient, pre-existing framework. In particular, the UFO phenomenon is still largely ignored by science although it has been a subject of persistent mystery for the last twenty-five years.

There is one haunting thought underlying the UFO phenomenon: *something* mysterious seems to be manifested in our environment—the "things" have been seen by thousands of people in all countries. They have been tracked on military radar, and they have been photographed by astronauts, leading many to the belief that they originated in outer space. They have been filmed by rocket-borne cameras and touched by farmers. They have been adored by simple people, denied by scientists, prayed to by the devout, cursed by primitives and celebrated by poets. They have been called Flying Saucer, Unidentified Flying Objects, Uncorrelated Targets.

This is not simply a book about UFOs or UCTs. This

book presents a personal interpretation of their patterns in the light of current changes in human consciousness. Basic to this interpretation is the fact that now, as at the end of the medieval era, there is a role to play for an Invisible College of scientists interested in totally new concepts.

The work of the Invisible College of UFO researchers is revolutionary because the scientists who compose it (about a hundred of them in five or six countries) are challenging accepted ideas in claiming that these strange observations deserve to be investigated and that no theory about them—no matter how fantastic by ordinary human standards—should be rejected without study. For a quarter of a century they have devoted their time and energy to this task. They have provided discreet support to groups of amateurs who have assembled the data that could not be obtained through official channels, and they have safeguarded these valuable records. Occasionally they have been able to keep the press and the public informed of the reality of the phenomena and of the existence of a serious—if inconspicuous—effort to understand it.

The research of the Invisible College has involved every available piece of scientific equipment—from flying-spot scanners to electronic microscopes—and much information of a remarkable nature has been found about the elusive "saucers." I was introduced to this informal group over ten years ago, when Dr. J. Allen Hynek, the U.S. Air Force's expert on UFO matters, invited me to apply my background in computer science to a study of the statistical procedures used by Project Blue Book. In the ensuing years I learned much about UFOs which was not then, and still is not now, public knowledge. I examined the 10,000 reports contained at that time in the files of the USAF, spending four years in sorting the signal from the noise. I visited the Foreign Technology Division of Wright-Patterson Air Force Base, where the Air Force centralized its "official" data. I found that frustration concerning this baffling problem was as high or even higher among military personnel as it was among the best informed of my scientific colleagues. And yet it did not seem that anything could be done to bring the facts into a sharper focus. Research went on slowly, and the reality of the problem was met day after day in the course of our quest.

As the significant facts were sorted out from the trivia, a strange and bewildering picture emerged: not only were the objects seen in the air, they were reported to land in the fields and on the roads of our planet. They affected the lives of human beings who found themselves close to them. A few of these witnesses gave stories to the press and were ridiculed. A much greater number never spoke at all. The scientists do not suspect, even now, to what extent the witnesses are reluctant to speak. They assume that there is nothing more to UFOs than what they occasionally read in the newspapers, and they feel justified in rejecting the whole thing.

Today the events I have been monitoring seem to have entered a phase that makes our methodology obsolete. The appearance on the scene of a few individuals with apparently abnormal abilities, like Uri Geller, who seeks and receives much publicity, and of others perhaps equally gifted, like my engineer friend, who wants absolutely to remain hidden, gives a new twist to this whole problem. It is not possible to study such data with the techniques of statistics or physics alone. The cooperation of a much larger group is needed, not as a new scientific society but as a growing community of people seriously considering and researching the subject. For this reason I have decided to place on record the facts and the issues as I have perceived them, hiding nothing of their complexity and stating what I think are their implications. And I propose the elements of a blueprint for a continued serious examination of the problem.

I cannot accept the idea (proposed by Dr. Puharich and others) that mankind is being psychically contacted by a benign intelligence from outer space. I do not believe Uri

Geller is a new Messiah. Neither can I believe my engineer friend when he tells me that according to the "teaching machine" the beings from outer space who fly the UFOs have no religion in the human sense and live in never-ending love, can make life longer and can replace any organ in the body. But how can I say that this man is a sincere witness, and yet reject his beliefs? This is one of the questions I think my book will answer.

I believe that a powerful force has influenced the human race in the past and is again influencing it now. Does this force originate entirely within human consciousness, or does it represent alien intervention? This is the question that forms the basis of the work of the Invisible College. And here is *what we know.*

San Francisco, California
March, 1975

CHAPTER ONE

The Psychic Component

In August of 1960 I witnessed the appearance of two UFOs and since that time have had occasional encounters with the phenomena. All of my experiences of this nature have been closely associated with psychic awareness in one form or another.

—letter from Mr. C., August 25, 1974

During the drive between Burford and Stratford I had some startling and, to me, novel insights into what I can only describe as the nature of reality. They were connected in some way to this shining disk, and have had a profound effect on me, causing what is commonly known as a personality change. I won't try to explain what those insights were since almost all the religions of the world have tried to do this and have failed.

—letter from Ms. U. December 13, 1973

Return of a Specter

It is difficult for the public to tolerate a mystery that refuses to die. When encounters with unidentified flying objects were suddenly reported all over the United States during the first half of October, 1973, and when two men from Pascagoula, Mississippi, told their tale of abduction by grotesque robot-like creatures, the public recognized the return of a specter that the good doctors of science had pronounced dead and buried with great pomp just a few years before. The burial had been performed by the University of Colorado at the cost of nearly half a million dollars, and the eight-hundred-page post-mortem had clearly stated that the study of UFOs "cannot be justified in the expectation that science will be advanced thereby." Professor Condon, who led the study, felt so strongly about the uselessness of the whole thing that he destroyed the project files. (Three days before his death, in March, 1974, he was still urging a physicist friend to drop his study of UFOs. When he was told that a documentary was being prepared he advocated that all the footage be burned.) The Air Force subsequently closed down its own public-relations office for the monitoring of sighting reports (Project Blue Book) with a similar declaration.

When the sightings exploded again in the world press, it became clear that the subject of UFOs was as alive as ever. It was easy for flying saucer enthusiasts everywhere to exclaim: "We told you so!" But it was not so easy for the witnesses to understand what they had seen. And it was even harder for them to forget it.

Some never will. A husband and wife team who drove a truck in the Midwest were fired from their job when they reported that an object had followed them along a Missouri road one October night, emitting a burst of light that blinded the husband (inducing some loss of eyesight, similar to the case of the engineer I have mentioned in the Introduction) and caused the plastic frame of his glasses to melt. Like the Pascagoula story of robot-like monsters, the facts were unbelievable to local scientists, who examined them out of the context of the overall phenomenon. Professor Condon had had the same problem: all the members of his team had been selected because they had no previous knowledge of the subject. Yet it is only when one analyzes the thousands of similar occurrences in the last twenty-five years and in all countries that one achieves some degree of understanding. My own statements here are based upon exactly such an analysis. We are looking at a phenomenon that many have thought dead because they have ignored the global nature of its manifestation.

In fact UFO activity has *not* abated in recent years. Even during the Colorado study, when investigators were at pains to find sightings in the United States, a large wave of observations was taking place in Spain and Portugal. The U.S. investigators never heard about these. In 1972 there was a peak of activity in Puerto Rico and many interesting cases took place in Western Europe. Interest was low among the news media, however, and the fact that the close encounters tend to take place in sparsely populated areas makes the study of these waves a difficult matter.

In recent years, too, the report of paranormal events in connection with close encounters with UFOs seems to have become the rule rather than the exception, and most investigators have found it very difficult to deal with this aspect of the cases. Such events might take the form of minor "unexplained coincidences" in which a man might have had a dream prior to the sighting (or heard a knock on the door and gone to open it, only to find no one was there, as happened to a policeman who later the same evening reported being paralyzed by two occupants of an unknown craft). Sometimes the event was more significant. A number of witnesses, for example, reported perceiving distinct "messages" inside their heads, a fact they interpreted as an indication of a telepathic ability on the part of the UFO occupants. Still other categories of psychic events are the distortions of time and space reported by witnesses and the apparent violations of physical laws represented by the sudden appearance and disappearance of physical craft. Close observers, like the engineer mentioned in the Introduction, have reported something akin to a trip into a parallel time-stream.

These observations constitute what I have termed the "psychic component" of the UFO phenomenon.

The aspect of the sightings that I find interesting is the very same aspect that has made scientists from other disciplines turn away in disgust; I am referring to their apparent *absurdity*. My field of research is the nature of information, its use by people, its transliteration in the form of documents, and its representation in the behavior of automata. By using the techniques of this field one can observe how major waves of UFO sightings (such as the 1973 wave in the U.S.) make an impact on our culture: they begin with a sudden series of impressive incidents which receive wide publicity; soon many people are excited and demand an explanation; every day the media report new cases; this period of acute activity may last from a period of a few weeks to three months.

When this initial phase is over, according to the patterns I have traced in previous periods, the genuine cases become adulterated with wishful thinking and fakes: some hoaxer confesses, or some photograph of a sky object enthusiastically carried on the front page of major newspapers is recognized as a picture of a weather balloon at sunset. The public laughs, and the wave of ridicule sweeps into oblivion hundreds of genuine sightings that deserved serious scrutiny. Then the task of compiling the observations, sorting them out, classifying them, and looking for patterns becomes a lonely one again. A few scientists are still pursuing this task in spite of the apparent absurdity of the data. Their work to unravel the UFO enigma centers increasingly on the psychic component of the reports, that aspect of many accounts that is indicative either of direct, extrasensory communication between the witness and the phenomenon or of direct influence of that phenomenon on the witness that is unexplainable by ordinary physical means.

Over the Accelerator

In the foothills of the California coastal range, just west of the city of Menlo Park where the Stanford linear accelerator plunges straight under the newly constructed expressway, there is a spot of unusual beauty. It is situated within a mile or so of a densely populated area, yet it gives one a feeling of utter loneliness; the linear accelerator stretches deep into this valley, guarded by wire fences, yet the fields around it have kept a sort of bucolic charm; where the accelerator ends there is a funnel-shaped depression which is not visible from the road. It is from that depression that a man saw an unusual object rise one evening in February, 1972.

The man was first attracted to the object by a humming sound it made (humming sounds, buzzing noises, and something compared to the swarming of bees are commonly reported as the auditory perception associated with a UFO). He stopped his car and he and his companion got out. The hum became more distinct as the object came into view. It was glowing red. It flew in a straight line, up the hill, as if following the roof of the elongated tunnel. Then it flew down again and was lost from sight in the valley. But not for long. It soon came back into view and this time it took off, rising very high and very fast as it passed overhead. The two men below saw it clearly: it was somewhat like looking directly at the sun, they said, although contours of the light were sharp. The impression was not like observing a strong projector attached to a flying object; it was more like looking through a window that "opened on the inside of a star."

The witness who told me this story mentioned having previously seen unidentified objects. On a certain occasion in Montana he had observed two disk-shaped craft crossing his path, and they had come to hover in a field. He walked toward them and approached within seventy-five feet. He had the intense feeling of being under observation, even at that distance. He used the word "communication."

"But how could you tell?" I asked him. "You have mentioned no window, no indication that there was life on these objects."

"Have you ever been close to a whale?" the witness asked me, implying that he had the vague feeling that the object somehow was aware of him, as a large animal is aware of the presence of a man while appearing to ignore him.

Do Not Report This!

Accounts such as the one I have just quoted abound in a corner of the psychic house that too few people interested in paranormal phenomena ever take the trouble to visit. In the last twenty-five years, at least five thousand sightings of unidentified flying objects have been filed away unexplained by competent investigators (I am not referring here to the number of cases *reported* but only to those *unsolved,* and my figure is a very conservative one), but no bridge has yet been built between this body of data and the evidence that exists for psychic phenomena such as psychokinesis, prophecy, and telepathy. Such a bridge is needed, not only because current research on parapsychology could help explain some of the more mystifying UFO incidents, but also because an understanding of the nature of the UFO phenomenon could provide new insights into unusual events that have not yet been duplicated in the laboratory, and would give a clue to the mechanism of some psychic processes.

The nature of the problem can be illustrated by another example, a report given to me by a woman living in Berkeley, California, who once observed a series of five round objects crossing the sky over East San Francisco Bay. She immediately thought they must be balloons. Then the first one accelerated and, upon reaching a certain spot, shot straight out of sight at an unbelievable speed. The second object did the same a few moments later while the other three continued. Then the third object dashed ahead and vanished in the sky. And the fourth, and finally the fifth. The sky was empty once again. But in the mind of the witness there was a strange thought, the strong suggestion that this "was all right for her to see." This was accompanied by another thought which almost came *as an explicit message:* This was nothing that she should report. And indeed she went home without breathing a word of the event to anyone, until she attended a lecture where I raised the question of the possibility of unconscious or repressed "contact." We will observe throughout this book how frequently witnesses decide to withhold this kind of information.

If we disregard the last part of the woman's testimony, she is simply another person among millions of Americans who believe that, at one time or another, they have seen a UFO. But do we have a right to disregard that section of her report? And what happens if we do take into consideration the fact that she distinctly felt a direct imperative message had been implanted in her mind, and that it was as much a part of the occurrence as her sensory observation of five luminous objects? What happens if we examine the files of UFO sightings with an open mind regarding such "psychic components"? We find that phenomena of precognition, telepathy, and even healing are not unusual among the reports, especially when they involve close-range observation of an object or direct exposure to its light.

The Case of Dr. X

The following case is among the most thoroughly investigated accounts of the interaction between human percipients (those who have "perceived" the phenomenon by whatever means) and the phenomenon of UFOs. It involved a medical doctor who holds an important official position in southern France. What is unusual about this case, which occurred the night of November 1–2, 1968, is the fact that competent investigators (including an astrophysicist, a psychiatrist and a physiologist) were able to

gain rapid access to the data and to monitor the development of subsequent events without interference from the
press or from military authorities. The witness wants absolutely no publicity in connection with his experiences:
neither his patients nor his immediate family know of the
events, which have been presented only in a British publication specialized in high-quality documentation of UFO
phenomena (The Flying Saucer Review, edited by Mr. C.
Bowen, c/o Compendium Books, 281 Camden High Street,
London NW1).

Shortly before 4 A.M. that night, the doctor was awak-
ened by the calls of his 14-month-old baby. Experiencing
some pain because three days earlier he had injured his
leg while chopping wood and still had a large haematoma
(an area of accumulated blood under the skin), he got up
and found the baby gesturing toward the window with excitement. Through the shutters, the doctor saw what he
first took to be flashes of lightning, but he paid little attention to this, gave a bottle of water to the baby, and went on
to inspect the house, for it was raining very hard (though
no thunder could be heard). The light flashes continued,
coming from the western part of the wide landscape that
can be seen from the south of the house, which is built on
the side of a hill. Opening a large window that leads onto
the terrace, the witness observed the objects for the first
time. There were two of them, disk-shaped, horizontal,
silvery-white on top and bright red underneath.

Other details of the objects that the doctor was later able
to recall include horizontal "antennae" and a vertical one
on top, while a beam of white light, perfectly cylindrical,
illuminated the mist under the disks. The flashes, which
occurred with a periodicity of about one second, were
marked by a brief increase in the luminosity of both disks,
followed by a sudden burst of light between them. The objects were moving in unison toward the left—that is to say,
toward the center of the doctor's field of view—and they
were coming closer, their apparent size increasing while

the object that seemed farthest away came to align itself with the closer one. While they were still approaching (following the trajectory of the beams on the ground enabled the witness to ascertain that they were indeed coming closer) these two disks went through a remarkable transformation: their "antennae" came into contact, the two beams interpenetrated, the flashing activity stopped, and the two craft *merged.*

There was now a single disk, directly facing the window and still coming nearer, with a single beam of white light underneath. After a time (the witness is unable to recall how long), the disk began flipping from a horizontal to a vertical position, until it was seen as a circle standing on edge. The shaft of light, which had been drawn by the rotation into a sweeping movement toward the house, came to illuminate the entire front and shone straight into the doctor's face. At that instant a "bang" was heard and the disk dematerialized, leaving behind a whitish glow which was slowly blown away by the wind.

I have summarized these events from an excellent report published in the *Flying Saucer Review*, reported by Mr. Aimé Michel, a science writer and a leading figure in the study of paranormal phenomena in France.

After these events the witness wrote a detailed account of his sighting, with sketches. He awoke his wife and told her what had happened. At that point it was she who observed, with considerable amazement, that *the swelling and pain in his leg had completely disappeared.* In the days that followed, he became aware that all the sequelae of a wound he had received during the Algerian war had also disappeared (he had suffered from right hemiparesis, a high degree of fatiguability on the right side, and pain while standing; he had been unable to keep his balance when standing on the right foot only). The reader should keep in mind the spontaneous healing of this man's leg. We shall have occasion to discuss it again in Chapter Seven.

Mr. Michel visited the witness on November 8, six days after the sighting, and found him tired; he had lost weight since the observation and was very much distressed by what had happened to him. That same day he experienced cramps and pains in the abdomen, and a red pigmentation appeared around the navel, forming a triangle. By November 17 this "preposterous" phenomenon was well-developed. Examinations by a dermatologist led to negative results, but the specialist was so intrigued by this triangular pigmentation without a cause that he decided to document it as a report to the French Academy of Medicine. The witness—who had not told the specialist that everything had started with his observation of a UFO—requested that on the contrary he give the phenomenon no publicity. During the night of November 13–14, the doctor had had a dream in which a triangular pattern was seen connected with a flying disk. The same triangle appeared on the baby's stomach a day or so after the witness' examination. The psychosomatic explanation first proposed by Aimé Michel had to be discarded.

When the investigator (who kept the witness under close observation) published the results of his two-year followup of the case, he noted that there had been no recurrence of either the war sequelae or the wound on the leg; the peculiar triangle, however, continued to come and go on both the father and the son, and would stay visible for two or three days at a time, even when the child was away and staying with his grandmother (who to this day knows nothing of the sighting and is very much alarmed when she sees the triangular pigmentation).

Like the grandmother, friends of the family still know nothing, but they have noted a change in the mental attitudes of the doctor and his wife: they seem to have acquired an almost mystical acceptance of the events of life and death, which is puzzling to those who had known them previously. Finally, there is the matter of the paranormal phenomena that now take place around them. Coincidences of a telepathic nature are frequently reported, and the doctor has even, on at least one occasion, experienced levitation without being able to control it. Clocks and electrical circuits have been affected, apparently without cause.

Such phenomena are not unprecedented. Cases of uncontrolled levitation or gravity effects have been reported in connection with UFOs. In one case, which took place in 1954 in the French countryside, a man who was coming back from the fields with his horse had to let go of the bridle as the animal was lifted several feet into the air—a dark, circular object was flying fast over the trail they were following.

Neither is the change in life patterns an uncommon fact among witnesses of close encounters with such objects. An awareness of the paranormal has been inspired by such sightings in men like Uri Geller and Edgar Cayce. The former's experiences are well known to many readers, but the latter's encounter may be less familiar. As a child, Edgar Cayce met a woman who appeared out of a sphere of radiant light and told him that he would be able to heal the sick when he grew up.

> As soon as the weather was good he went back to his retreat in the woods. There, one afternoon in May . . . he became aware of the presence of someone else. He looked up. A woman was standing before him. . . . "Your prayers have been heard," she said, "tell me what you would like most of all, so that I may give it to you." "Most of all I would like to be helpful to others, and especially to children when they are sick." Suddenly she was no longer there. He looked at the place where she had stood, trying to see her in the beams of light, but she was gone.[1]

Edgar Cayce's sighting is reminiscent of several cases that fall into the category of religious experiences, al-

1. Thomas Sugrue, *There Is a River* (New York: Dell paperback, 1970), p. 45.

though the initial observation is often linked to an unusual
flying object, as in the "miracles" of Lourdes and Fatima,
which we will analyze in Chapter Seven, and in the visions that led to the founding of the Mormon church. It is
noteworthy that such "miracles" often give to the percipients healing or prophetic powers. In the case of Uri Geller, who, like the French doctor, traces his paranormal
abilities to his exposure to a peculiar beam of light that
came from the sky, we have an example of psychokinetic
phenomena where the "sensitive" believes the source of
his power to be an extraterrestrial one. In the concluding
section of this chapter we will have occasion to question
this interpretation, but it is already clear that such statements place the problem of "contact" in a totally new
framework.

Meta-Logic

What do we know of the nature of the communication that
is reported to occur between human witnesses and the
UFOs they perceive? I have earlier commented that, on
the surface, such communication appears to be simply absurd. The word "absurd," however, is misleading; I prefer
the expression "meta-logical." When a witness meets a
UFO occupant who asks, "What time is it?" and replies,
"It's 2:30," only to be bluntly told, "You lie—it is 4
o'clock" (this actually happened in France in 1954), the
story is not simply absurd. It has a symbolic meaning
beyond the apparent contradiction of the dialogue. Could
it be that the true meaning of the dialogue is "time is not
what you think it is," or "any measurement of time can
only be relative"? In 1961, similarly, Barney Hill found
himself trying to explain to the humanoid examining him
that time was an important concept for us on earth. The
humanoid appeared not to understand what he meant. In
an even more remarkable case in South America, a man
who found himself inside a UFO could see the "pilots"

consulting a device contained in a box. He managed to look into this box and saw what looked like a clock, but the clock had no hands. The point of these incidents seems to have been to convey the fact that consciousness transcended time itself.

Situations such as these often have the deep poetic and paradoxical quality of Eastern religious tales ("What is the sound of one hand clapping?") and the mystical expressions of the Cabala, such as references to a "dark flame." If you strive to convey a truth that lies beyond the semantic level made possible by your audience's language, you must construct apparent contradictions in terms of ordinary meaning. In the above contact case in France, the next question was about *space,* and again was absurd ("Am I in Italy or Germany?" asked the UFO pilot). What scientist would take such a story seriously? What public official would risk his reputation by reacting in earnest? Even a priest might avoid it, for fear of demons! In fact, some witnesses have thought they had seen demons because the creature had the unpredictability and mischievousness associated with popular conceptions of the devil. If you wanted to bypass the intelligentsia and the Church, remain undectectable to the military system, and leave undisturbed the political and administrative levels of a society, and at the same time implant deep within that society far-reaching doubts concerning its basic philosophical tenets, this is exactly how you would have to act. At the same time, of course, such a process *would have to provide its own explanation* to make ultimate detection impossible. In other words, it would have to project an image just beyond the belief structure of the target society. I think the current belief among most flying saucer enthusiasts that the unidentified flying objects are simply craft used by visitors from another planet is a naïve concept. The explanation is too simpleminded to account for the diversity of the reported behavior of the occupants and their perceived interaction with human beings. Could this concept serve precisely a diversionary role in masking the real, infinitely more complex nature of the technology that gives rise to the sightings?

Observations similar to the landing at Pascagoula (where two fishermen claimed to have been abducted by "clawmen") have been made every year in the United States since 1947. A computer catalogue of close encounter cases which I am compiling for purposes of content analysis will hold the details of nearly two thousand cases of that type, from all countries, indicating that a formidable impact is being made on our collective psyche. Yet what trace has this produced on scientific patterns? A very small one indeed: a few courageous astronomers are beginning to revise the probability estimates for other civilizations in space; much is made of the possibility of detecting radio signals from other solar systems; and a few physicists are timidly beginning to voice their doubts concerning Dr. Condon's biases. Against such a background I am afraid that my own speculations will contradict both the ideas of the believers and the assumptions of the skeptics. I would not feel justified in offering them here if I had not had the opportunity to discuss them privately with professional scientists forming the Invisible College of UFO research. All have encouraged me to share these speculations with a wider public, in the hope that some piece of the puzzle, as yet undisclosed, may come to light.

Five Statements

Here, then, is a necessarily brief statement of five useful propositions:

1. The things we call unidentified flying objects are neither objects nor flying. They can dematerialize, as some recent photographs show, and they violate the laws of motion as we know them.

2. UFOs have been seen throughout history and have consistently received (or provided) their own explanation

within the framework of each culture. In antiquity their occupants were regarded as gods; in medieval times, as magicians; in the nineteenth century, as scientific geniuses. And finally, in our own time, as interplanetary travelers. (Statements made by occupants of the 1897 airship included such declarations as "We are from Kansas" and even "We are from ANYWHERE . . . but we'll be in Cuba tomorrow.")

3. UFO reports are not necessarily caused by visits from space travelers. The phenomenon could be a manifestation of a much more complex technology. If time and space are not as simple in structure as physicists have assumed until now, then the question, "where do they come from?" may be meaningless: they could come from a place in *time*. If consciousness can be manifested outside the body, then the range of hypotheses can be even wider.

4. The key to an understanding of the phenomenon lies in the psychic effects it produces (or the psychic awareness it makes possible) in its observers. Their lives are often deeply changed, and they develop unusual talents with which they may find it difficult to cope. The proportion of witnesses who do come forward and publish accounts of these experiences seems to be quite low; most of them choose to remain silent.

5. Contact between human percipients and the UFO phenomenon occurs under conditions controlled by the latter. Its characteristic feature is a constant factor of absurdity that leads to a rejection of the story by the upper layers of the target society and an absorption at a deep unconscious level of the symbols conveyed by the encounter. The mechanism of this "resonance" between the UFO symbol and the archetypes of the human unconscious has been abundantly demonstrated by Carl Jung, whose book, *Flying Saucers*, makes many references to the age-old significance of the "signs in the sky."

I am not regarding the phenomenon of the UFOs as the unknowable, uncontrollable game of a higher order of beings. Neither is it likely, in my view, that an encounter with them would add to the human being anything it did not already possess—at an unconscious level, possibly. Everything works, in my opinion, as if the phenomenon were the product of a *technology* that followed well-defined rules and patterns, though fantastic by ordinary human standards. The phenomenon has so far posed no apparent threat to national defense and seems to be indifferent to the welfare of individual witnesses, leading many to assume that we may be dealing with a still-undiscovered natural occurrence ("It cannot be intelligent"—say these people—"because it does not attack us!"). But its impact in shaping man's long-term creativity and unconscious impulses is probably enormous. The fact that we have no methodology to deal with such an impact is only an indication of how little we know about our own psychic world.

Aveyron, or the Essence of Prophecy

Two well-investigated cases of recent years have contained psychic elements. One took place in Aveyron, France, and the other one in Kansas.

On June 15, 1966, in Aveyron (a region of France situated near the mid-Pyrenees) a 76-year-old woman made the first in a long and fascinating series of sightings that centered on an isolated farm. The farmhouse itself is very old, with ten rooms whose windows face south and command an excellent view.

> I was at the window—just for a moment—because at my age you need a breath of air wherever you are. But never have I seen lights like that, nor things like that! They weren't just lights, they were fires!

The old woman became fearful, and the words she used to describe her anguish convey the precise feeling that many witnesses have tried to express in all languages:

All these fires—I'm too old, I don't want to see things
like that. If this thing's going to move about like that,
what's to become of us all? Afterwards it moved again,
over by the corner of the vineyard, you remember
[speaking to her son-in-law], that's when I called you,
that's when I was frightened, but if that comes any
closer, that's going to go in the barn and everything will
go up in smoke, the house and us with it—so I called
him, I called him.

Mr. Fernand Lagarde, who conducted a very thorough
investigation of the events, reports in his summary (published in *Flying Saucer Review* Sep./Oct., 1970) that "the
haunting thought of fire frightens all country people, and
so, distracted and scared, she calls her son-in-law to help,
and later she will tell us that she went to bed fully clothed,
for fear of what might be to come. This is a story with all
the ring of truth about it."

The fiery objects are in fact spherical in shape, and they
cross the fields with deliberate motion. The son-in-law,
who works the farm, also observed what the old woman
has seen, and goes out to investigate. The objects, he says,
are rounded on top and rather flattened underneath, and
they vanish on the spot as if controlled by a switch. At one
point there are six of them, less than a mile away; they
move in one line at the speed of a tractor, and they enter a
larger luminous object that appears as a sort of fiery tree,
an illuminated shell. Everything disappears, and the witnesses retire in complete puzzlement.

This feeling was still very clear in the taped interviews
that I heard during a recent trip to France, and Mr.
Lagarde confirmed that everything appeared to them dis-
concerting and irrational. It went on "in the calm night,
without a sound, unreal and dreamlike." The luminous
spheres came back to the farm in Aveyron six months
later—on January 6, 1967, to be exact. The farmer had
gone out to check on the animals when he suddenly saw
one sphere not more than fifty yards away. He decided to

"get round behind that thing to see what it is," having assumed that "it" had a front and a back, but when he got outside the gate, the sphere was next to it, waiting for him. He had left it inside the yard a moment before. The man then decided to take a small path through the fields and again get behind that object, but the sphere proceeded to follow him over about sixty yards, and went to block the entrance to the path!

> That there thing followed me for about 60 metres, near enough . . . and then there was a narrow bit where I wanted to get through, I did . . . so's to get round behind, then "that" followed me right along, right along . . . till I stopped there, where I wanted to get round behind, and the "machine" stops there too, right at the narrow bit. So I says, now . . . 'tain't no use to argue. . . . I can't get past!

Coming back into the house, the farmer called his son, and going outside they saw six spheres this time, and were so afraid that they went back inside the house. The larger shell-shaped object was there, too, and it was giving off a beam of light, as a searchlight would:

> There was a searchlight on top, right at the end of it, and it lit up that window up there, lit up the whole room it did. . . . I had the window open there opposite.
> Was it a diffused beam, or rather very concentrated?
> Oh, concentrated, very concentrated.
> And it lit up your room?
> Yes, lit it up all right . . . off and on like . . . it was turning . . . kept on turning.
> It was turning round and round, like a beacon?
> Yes, sometimes it lit up the next room down there . . . kept on turning around . . . but there it was, 23:00 already, maybe 23:15, something like that.
> Then, sudden-like, everything died out. It all died out, and I didn't see anything more. I don't know if it had gone, or if it was still there.

The culmination of the series of sightings in Aveyron, which I am merely summarizing here, took place on January 11, 1967, when the son saw the "shell" coming down near the house. He drove near it and could see that it was very large indeed. Two of the smaller spheres entered it, then it became very bright and the witness heard a whistling sound. It tilted at a 45-degree angle and was gone at an incredible speed.

Another object came. It was shaped like a disk, with two transparent cupolas on top of it, and inside . . .

> Well now, inside . . . it seemed to me to be lit up inside with a green light . . . inside the two domes . . . and I saw . . . mind you I can't be sure about this . . . it was very dark, you might have said there was some sort of fog, either inside or outside . . . don't know which . . . inside or outside the two domes. Anyway I thought I saw two . . . well, I saw two people like . . . human beings, see? . . . Cosmonauts. They wore overalls like aircrew, green trimmed with white.

The object itself was hovering, with a motion forward and back, pitching and rolling. The investigator asked more questions:

> Did you have the car doors shut during this time?
> Yes, yes . . . I must have opened the window, I think.
> . . . Or perhaps it was afterwards, when it went off, that I opened the window . . . and then I felt a wave of heat, and I felt myself almost . . . I couldn't move hand or foot, for as long as it lasted.

After about a week, the witness began to have trouble with his sleeping habits. He would sleep as much as twenty hours a day, and in spite of his parents' advice he didn't want to consult a doctor. He simply couldn't stay on his feet when it hit him, and this went on for about two months. Something else happened to him in connection

with his sleeping pattern: in the early morning hours, between 4 and 5 A.M., it seemed to him that he was "floating
off." His mind would be alert, although his body was paralyzed, and he would feel his consciousness leaving his
body.

In later conversations with the investigators I learned
several facts that they regard as outside the scope of the
UFO phenomenon itself; these facts will be seen to be in
the perspective of the present approach, however, when I
mention that they involve changes in the witness' behavior and belief system; these changes take the form of a
new awareness of the world around him. He surprised everyone in this remote area of France by recommending to
young people that they study astronomy and science in
general with great care; and in a private discussion with
one of the researchers who have for several years followed
up this remarkable case, he casually mentioned that he
might soon have to write a book. It was pointed out to him
that he could hardly write even the most simple letter.
"THEY told me not to worry about that," he said! "When
the time is right, I will know what to put on paper."

We are touching here the very essence of prophecy.

"THEY" told him. . . . But who are THEY? It seems
that, in recurrent dreams since the incident with the flying
disk, he has seen a number of men, dressed in red, and
each holding a book and pointing at it. Nothing else happens in the dream. Just the men, and the book.

More recently he has traveled over two hundred miles
to visit the investigator, who had left precise instructions
to keep him closely informed of any new and important
development. But when he was in the investigator's house
he could not talk. The part of his brain that handled verbal
expression and the mechanism of language could not process the data that he knew were there. We will come back
again to this type of effect in the course of this book. We
have much new and exciting ground to cover. From
Aveyron to Uri Geller, something is happening to human

consciousness. We see it again in a case that took place in the U.S.

The Delphos Case

In the evening of November 2, 1971, on the Johnson farm located near Delphos, Kansas, eleven miles South of Minneapolis, an unknown object was reported to come down almost to ground level and took off again. It was seen by a young man and later by his parents, and it would simply have gone into the annals of ufology as one of many thousands of "landings" if it had not been for several secondary effects the object created: it affected animals; it left peculiar traces on the ground; and, as in the French case of Aveyron, it affected the witness' sleeping pattern.

Here again the young son of the farmer is the main witness. Sixteen-year-old Ronald Johnson, was tending the sheep, accompanied by his dog, when it happened. What they suddenly saw was a mushroom-shaped object, illuminated by multicolored lights over its entire surface, and hovering within two feet of the ground twenty-five yards away. Its diameter was about nine feet.

The glow from the object was such that he could see no details, and it was making a sound like "an old washing machine which vibrates." Then it brightened at the base and took off. The witness reportedly became temporarily blind. During all this the dog was "very quiet."

After several minutes Ronald, regaining his sight, ran into the house to call his parents, and all came out again to see the object, now high in the sky and over half the full moon in size. It vanished into the distance.

The three witnesses went around the house to the site of the near landing and were surprised, they said, to observe a glowing ring on the ground. Parts of nearby trees were also glowing. The texture of the soil, reports an investigator, Mr. Ted Phillips, "felt strange, like a slick crust, as if the soil was crystallized." And Mrs. Johnson noticed that her fingers went numb, as if a local anesthetic had been applied. She is a nurse at a nearby hospital, and for two weeks this condition prevented her from taking the pulse of her patients.

The next day the ring was still clearly visible, with a dry and "crusty" appearance. The inside and the outside of the ring were damp from recent rains, but the ring itself was perfectly dry! Thirty-two days later, when Ted Phillips was able to go to the scene, snow had fallen and was melting both outside and inside the ring, but the one-foot wide circle was perfectly white.

> We removed snow from one section of the ring and in-troduced water into the exposed ring area: the soil would not permit the water to pass through the surface. This was most remarkable, as there had been several inches of rain and snow.[2]

Phillips removed a sample from the ring and observed that it contained a high concentration of a whitish material. The soil under the ring was dry to a depth of at least one foot.

This is not an isolated occurrence. Hundreds of reports of ring-shaped patterns have been gathered, and many of them refer to a white substance or powder at the site. A very similar occurrence took place in New Zealand, at a place named Waihoke, in January, 1965. The ring there was visible for four years before it was finally covered with grass. It is curious that in spite of all the excitement caused by the Delphos case and the attention it received from "scientific" ufologists and from skeptics, *no one ever bothered to identify the white substance itself.* Thorough analyses of the soil have been made, however, showing no significant difference between the inside and the outside of the ring. I obtained a sample of the white substance from Mr. Phillips and forwarded it to a biological labora-

2. Case Histories, *Flying Saucer Review* (February, 1972).

tory in France, where it was examined under a microscope with magnifications ranging from a few diameters to the maximum enlargement possible under the oil immersion technique. The white substance was resolved into fibers (thus destroying the "explanation" of the case put forth by Philip Klass in his book *UFOs Explained,* where he claimed the substance was produced by the urine of sheep feeding from a circular device). The fibers were vegetal in nature and belonged to an organism of the order of the Actinomycetales, which is an intermediate organism between bacteria and fungus. (The French biologist who identified it, and who has wished not to be named in this book determined that the organism belongs to the family of the Actinomycetaceae and the genus "Nocardia.") It is often found together with a fungus of the order of the Bacidiomycepes, which may fluoresce under certain conditions. This fungus can cause a circular pattern to be visible on the surface of the ground. This is undoubtedly the explanation for some UFO "rings," but the coincidence of this fungus ring with the observation made by the Johnsons remains to be explained. One possible interpretation is that high-energy stimulation triggered the spectacular growth of the Nocardia and of an existing fungus and caused the latter to fluoresce. If this is the case, then further examination of the white fibers might give a clue to the physical nature of the phenomenon.

The effects of the glowing object on animals were consistent with other landing cases. During the sighting itself, the dog was very quiet: he did not move at all nor did he bark. The sheep were bellowing, but like the dog they were almost glued to the spot. The boy could not move either, but it was not clear to him whether this was due to fear or to another cause. The behavior of the animals after the sighting was remarkable. For about two weeks, every evening at sunset, the sheep would jump out of the pen and run wildly. The dog would furiously try to get into the house at nightfall. He practically destroyed the screen door, and the only way to keep him outside was to replace it with a stronger metal door.

There were striking effects on the witness himself, too. First he suffered from strong eye irritation—his eyes were red and watery. Then came the headaches, and the nightmares. These nightmares, lasting about one week, were so real and vivid that he would wake up his parents with his loud screams. He had the same dream, night after night, in which human-like creatures were looking into his window from the outside. Two or three times, when coming into his bedroom, his parents found him screaming, standing by the window.

CHAPTER TWO

The Triple Coverup

We are pleased to acknowledge receipt of your letter
. . . regarding the photographs showing UFOs in forma-
tional flight, which you mention were taken by Captain
Orrego of the Chilean Navy near Antarctica in 1948.
   Regarding this matter we wish to inform you that recently we received a communication from Captain Orrego stating that he had not seen any UFOs over the Antarctica in 1948. Therefore the photographs requested by
you do not exist.

> —Letter from the Chief of the Chilean
> Naval Mission to an American writer

It is forbidden for T.V., radio, newspapers, and other
news media to divulge UFO reports without the prior
censorship of the Brazilian Air Force.

> —Institutional Act No. 5,
> State Security,
> Brazilian Government Regulation

Credibility Gap

In 1971, after an unusual UFO sighting, several puzzling
objects fell from the sky. These mysterious fragments were
picked up by a Texan who showed them to his friends.
The next day two men from Air Force Intelligence came to
his door, exhibited their identification papers, and politely
requested the evidence. The witness threw them out

rudely with a statement that I find admirable: "God has made everything in this world, and He has made Flying Saucers too, whatever they are. These fragments have fallen into my backyard and therefore God clearly intended for me to have them. If He had wanted the Air Force to have them, He would have dumped them on the Pentagon!"

In a recent survey of technically trained witnesses who had seen an unidentified flying object, it was found that the proportion of those who had bothered to call the Air Force was only one in twelve! This attitude toward the authorities is an important component of the UFO phenomenon. It enables the idea of a cosmic mystery to linger in the more shadowy areas of our imagination, and thus to influence much more powerfully our collective behavior, reflected in treatment of UFO stories in the media and in books. Could it be that our reaction to the reports, individually and collectively, is as much a part of the UFO phenomenon as the objects themselves? In the first chapter we discussed the psychic component of the UFO phenomenon. Now we must look at the chaotic reaction of our official levels confronted by this mystery, resulting in the existence of three levels of coverup.

The First Coverup

The first level of coverup is in the reporting of UFOs. It is the result of the negative attitude of government, scientific, and military authorities. More specifically, I apply the expression "first coverup" to the efforts that are made by men in a position of authority to discourage the reporting of a UFO incident. This can range from the laughter of a local deputy sheriff to intimidation of pilots by their commanding officer. In some cases the public is led to believe that reporting UFOs is unnecessary because the government knows all about them. An indication that official statements about UFOs were biased and deliberately inac-

curate came to my attention in 1964. Until then, I had naturally been aware of the strange games played by officials
who were trying to explain UFOs at all costs. Such games
had been put forth in several books claiming that the U.S.
government knew everything about the reality of the saucers. However, I had not seen any direct evidence that
confirmed these claims either in my contacts with the Air
Force or with scientific colleagues.

Late in 1964, several friends in Paris sent me interesting
data. It seems that somebody there was trying to spread
UFO-related stories through the French news media (the
French word for such spreading of rumors is "intoxica-
tion"). A former member of the Intelligence Service, for
instance, who was regarded as a "reliable source," made
statements to the effect that the British military was carefully monitoring the UFO situation and was pooling its information with the Russians! The idea seemed preposterous, but he offered it in all seriousness and went on to
say that both countries had now come to the conclusion
that the objects were real. Another story that circulated
among Paris newsmen came from an American who
claimed that federal law enforcement agencies had com-
piled exhaustive studies of the U.S. cases, a rumor that appears at least partially true, because some landing cases
have had elements that brought the event within the juris-
diction of these agencies.

In both of these stories, which originated from quasi-of-
ficial sources, there was the same reassuring theme: people should not worry about UFOs and should leave the investigation in the hands of the competent authorities, who
knew everything there was to know. We were well pro-
tected.

In the meantime I was observing a very different situation and a state of mounting uneasiness among the scientists who had been involved, even remotely, in the UFO
debate. Observations were not simply coming from
farmers and truck drivers but from jet pilots, and oc-

casionally from a grave professor or two. In August, 1965, Colonel Spaulding made inquiries among top scientists associated with his office at the Air Force. He asked them specifically what they thought of submitting the UFO files to the Academy of Sciences or to some such highly respected body, in an effort to reassure the public.

Early in November, 1965, the Scientific Advisory Board of the Air Force met in Dallas and discussed the UFO question. The idea of an "independent" study was first considered at that meeting. It eventually led to the Condon investigation. A physicist, Dr. Brien O'Brien, headed a special study group that came back with the recommendation that the Air Force spend $250,000 a year to obtain "high-grade data." The very fact that a new study was recommended seems to show that any suppression of information or any leaking of wild rumors was not the result of a secret military policy on the UFO subject or the work of a sinister "Silence Group" but more likely a product of the confusion that was evident at all levels of the bureaucracy. The military was reacting to the sightings in direct proportion to their impact on the press, which they were trying to minimize, and these reactions were clumsy. The confusion that resulted was unbelievable. The best example of this was the Swamp Gas crisis.

Swamp Gas

The Swamp Gas episode has been told many times, and I do not intend to devote a great deal of space to it here. The fact is that, for better or worse, it played a decisive role in influencing public opinion and so it provides a model for local and national passion that we should keep in mind. The Swamp Gas crisis began for me on Monday morning, March 21, 1966. I was listening to a Chicago radio program when the news of the then recent Michigan sightings was broadcast: four objects were said to have flown over a farm near Ann Arbor, and one of them had landed in a swampy area. It sounded fairly typical. In 1964 I had established that landings tended to occur in desolate places, a fact that was first apparent in the computer analysis of French cases. Allen Hynek and I later verified it, using Air Force data. Swamps like the Everglades region of Florida were among the places that UFOs seemed to prefer. In 1965 there had been a series of reports by Australian farmers describing craft that left circular traces in the vegetation covering the swamps there. People had even created a new expression, "UFO nests," to describe these markings.

I called Dr. Hynek to alert him to the sightings, and he in turn called Project Blue Book in Dayton, Ohio, to propose that they investigate at once. He suggested that he go there before reporters and curiosity-seekers destroyed all the evidence. The officer in Dayton was not interested, as Allen Hynek later told me:

> The case hasn't been reported officially to the Air Force, he said.
> That's not very scientific, Hynek remarked.
> I don't give a damn, was the literal answer.

Half an hour later, Project Blue Book called back:

> How soon can you be in Ann Arbor?
> I thought you weren't interested!
> Well, someone has reported the case officially to us just a minute ago.
> Who was that?
> The Pentagon! They are deluged with calls. Every reporter in the country wants to know what's going on.

The next morning, Dr. Hynek was in Michigan. What happened in Ann Arbor is a classic example of misunderstanding with the press; Hynek had to release a statement prematurely, at the urging of public-relations people from the Air Force. In his statement, he called for a thorough investigation of the phenomenon, but mentioned also that *some* people in Michigan *might* have seen swamp gas. The press took this for a final verdict and exploded with anger. How dare this academic man from Chicago challenge the word of an honest farmer and seriously suggest that he had not seen what was evidently a real flying saucer?

Those irate comments came from the same newspapers who for years had ridiculed witnesses just like this poor farmer, and had given no support whatsoever to Hynek himself when he begged them to report UFO cases more regularly and more accurately. Suddenly it had become fashionable to believe in flying saucers, just as tomorrow it will perhaps be fashionable to believe in UMMO, AFFA, or SPECTRA, or any of the mysterious entities that we will investigate in the next few chapters. In March, 1966, newsmen were beating the bushes of Michigan looking for Martians and UFO experts. The switch took the Air Force by surprise and destroyed the image of Project Blue Book in a few short days.

Public reaction following the swamp gas statement carried the case to Washington, with help from a then local politician, Gerald Ford, who demanded that full attention be given to what had become known as the Swamp Gas scandal. A meeting of the space committee of the Senate pondered the question first and decided that NASA should not get involved. The space agency had its public image to preserve and declined to have anything to do with the subject. So they handed this hot potato to the armed forces committee of the House.

Early in April, 1966, the Secretary of the Air Force was himself reported to be in favor of a scientific analysis of the 648 cases that were classified as "unidentified" at that time in the Blue Book files. Late that month, the governor of Florida and several newsmen saw an unknown flying object from the governor's private plane. These reports created a stir, but the outrage over the Michigan incident had already subsided. It was almost two months old and no longer newsworthy. The public-relations people in Washington knew this well. On television a beautiful documentary was released, carrying the debunking of the subject to new heights: it showed astronomer Donald Menzel pouring some benzine over a tankful of acetone to demonstrate optical properties that were common knowledge since the eighteenth century. He was trying to convince the audience that UFO's were nothing but mirages.

"Let me know next time it rains benzine, will you?" I asked my wife. "We'll go out and watch the flying saucers!"

Menzel's number was followed by a classic interview with a "contactee" who was relied upon to provide comic relief by describing his meetings with the "space brothers." His statements were carefully chosen, possibly out of hours of interviews, to make him look as silly as possible. In contrast with this man, the next interview was a very impressive discussion with another astronomer who stated with authority that extraterrestrial visitations were most improbable. What he knew well, and did not say, is that he was merely offering a statistical estimate whose reliability was totally unverifiable. He fell victim to the faulty reasoning: "Either it's all nonsense or we are visited by beings from another planet."

The documentary also contained an interview with a military officer who stated that no UFOs were ever detected on radar screens, and an interview of an astronomer who declared that no UFOs were ever seen or photographed by the satellite tracking stations. Both statements were, in my opinion, misleading. It is true that radars never "see" UFOs, but that is only due to the fact that the radar operators call them something else! In their jargon they speak of UCTs, for "uncorrelated targets"! At the time when the documentary was shown, the Western Defense System was recording about seven hundred of these baffling UCTs *per month!* There had even been a suggestion by a highly respected astronomer that the military modify their computer program to gather information about these UCTs rather than ignoring them because they didn't fit the trajectory of incoming rockets. Even coming from such a source as this, the suggestion was not implemented.

In a letter to a scientist who had investigated a certain UFO sighting in 1953, a witness wrote, *thirteen years* later:

> I was told in 1953 to not reveal any facts about this case and have rigidly maintained my secrecy through the years. To be perfectly frank I'd just as soon not become involved again but . . . if you think it might possibly do some good, I will . . . try to reveal what I remember. . . . It has been my personal observation that whenever anyone mentions having seen a UFO, the general public is inclined to nod their head, smile wryly and mention something about "candidates to the funny farm."

Scared Scientists

Why were the scientists remaining silent? Many astronomers must have known what I knew from my days at Paris Observatory, namely that we were tracking unidentified objects, and even photographing them. There were films, too. Were professional scientists afraid of the emotional reaction their statements might trigger in a generally uninformed and credulous public? Was it due to their desire to avoid making statements before all the facts were in? Whatever the reason, it could not really justify the deliberate destruction of scientific data. Even the idea of "not saying anything that might cause fear" did not hold water. The Michigan incident proved that fear could spread much faster, and with much more destructive effects, among a population that had been kept systematically ignorant of the facts. Child psychologists know very well that it is better to prepare the child for the idea that his grandfather is not going to live forever than to let him discover it when death suddenly strikes. Similarly, by denying the existence of the mystery the scientific community was taking serious chances with the belief system of the public. In my opinion, such attitudes have contributed to the long-term loss of popular support and popular respect for science.

Much was happening under the surface. Several scientists who had been associated with the UFO field through periodicals or books began receiving letters and phone calls from specialists who wanted to participate in the investigation of the phenomenon. In his absorbing book *The UFO Experience* Dr. Hynek has described how this little group grew during the late sixties. If this network ever decided to become visible, a very brilliant panel of scientists could rapidly be assembled from its ranks to deal effectively with this new area of research. Given current conditions, however, it is probably best for these men to take few chances and to continue their investigations in private. The history of the Condon investigation at the University of Colorado convinced many of us of this fact.

What Condon Didn't Know

My own theory of the Condon fiasco is not a coverup scenario. I believe that the Air Force late in 1966 was simply fed up.

After over twenty years of analysis of this problem, the military was in essence saying to academia, with good reason, we have found no evidence that it lies within our mission to solve it. The objects are not openly behaving as enemies of the United States. We do not even know what they are made of, and every time we submit a case to the scientists they ridicule our pilots, who are only guilty of trusting their own eyes and their own instruments. We have had enough of this. Here are the data. It is your turn to see what you can make of these phenomena.

The scientific community, which had been so eager to make statements before the cameras to explain UFOs, as long as the Air Force was in charge, reacted coolly to the suggestion that their explanations should perhaps be tested on a larger scale. Several universities were contacted by the Department of Defense but they turned down the assignment. (This must have caused great anguish to the administrators of these universities at a time when half a million dollars would have come in quite handy.)

Some Europeans followed this development with keen interest. The British had adopted an attitude of quiet reserve, but in France there was an eager expectation of the American decision: official French policy would be modeled after the U.S. stand on the matter. There was explosive material in the European files. Many of the sightings were extremely well documented, and investigations of the highest caliber had been made much more thoroughly and professionally than even the best cases in the Air Force files. And no wonder. Some of the witnesses had been of the highest political rank. In one European country, *a near landing had taken place on the Chief of State's private estate!* The craft had been described in detail by members of the official's entourage. This meant that the observation had not been studied by the local police, or even by trusted scientists; the investigation had been conducted at the very top level by secret service experts. The chauffeur of this high political authority, as described in a report of the sighting, while driving through the estate,

> sees what he believes to be an aircraft trying to land on the road, directly in front of him. He stops the car immediately. The object passes just a few meters above the stopped car and, while doing this, causes violent vertical vibrations in the vehicle. A few seconds later, the object reverses its course and passes again, now in the opposite direction, with the same effects on the car. Then, having regained its position above some trees where it had ini-

tially appeared, it makes a fast change of altitude, a ninety-degree tilting with respect to the horizontal, and darts away to the west.

The witness is highly reliable [the report goes on]. We found that the object, an upside-down plate with a central turret and portholes, could be of the dimensions reported by the witness, namely twenty meters.

Such an observation was no joke. Neither the U.S. Air Force nor the American academic community was aware of the extent of the problem in Western Europe. The Soviets were possibly even more interested than the West Europeans.

The rumor that spread in Europe through "informal channels" during the summer of 1966 was a difficult one to verify, but in view of later events in the history of the Condon Committee it has some interest. According to that rumor, the Air Force was completely frustrated with the UFO problem and was looking for an excuse to get rid of it. The only problem was to find a university that was willing to write a negative report after a cursory examination of the facts. This, I repeat, was only a rumor. But this rumor was taken seriously enough in Paris to prevent the creation of an investigation committee similar to the American one. The Russians made some moves toward the creation of a committee but cleverly awaited the developments in the U.S. before funding it and giving it an official stamp of approval. In Boulder, Colorado, a group was finally being assembled with much fanfare, headed by Dr. Condon, a prestigious physicist close to retirement. The group had received a sizable grant to ponder ufology and its report was due in 1969. It would prove to be negative.

Destroying the Data

In November, 1966, when the Colorado Committee started gathering testimony from people who had done research into UFO cases, Dr. Hynek and I traveled to Boulder to brief the Condon group. We noticed that one of the administrators was clearly the decision-maker in the team although he had no science degree and little interest in the whole matter. There was a certain euphoric feeling in the room, a sense of embarking on a unique adventure. There was little passion in the press now; the Michigan crisis had been largely forgotten. The problem was in the hands of the scientists and it had become as dull as any venture that is in the process of being rationalized away by the academic mill. If the journey to the moon can be turned into the exasperating bore that modern technology has generated, there is no reason to expect that the same lack of interest will not settle over the UFO mystery once it falls into the hands of Big Science! (The first astronauts to die in space will probably die of ennui when they run out of buttons to push, digits to read out, and jokes about the football scores.)

As early as February, 1967, members of the Condon Committee were privately approaching their scientific colleagues on other campuses, asking them how they would react if the committee's final report to the Air Force were to recommend closing down Project Blue Book. A few months later the work of the committee had come to a standstill. Field investigations were nonexistent. Questionnaires were sent out to witnesses, but only one assistant was available to encode the results for the computer file, where the bulk of the information was provided by the three thousand punched cards I had turned over to the committee.

A minority faction of the group caused a crisis when they rebelled. After a series of incidents that Dr. Saunders has documented in an excellent book, *UFOs? Yes!*, the team split into two violently opposed factions. An early internal memorandum was discovered and published by the minority group as evidence that the Condon Committee had never intended to look seriously into the UFO problem. Publication of this document so outraged Condon that he fired the minority group and ran the project without serious consideration of the possible reality of the phenomenon.

The files of Project Blue Book have now been transferred into the Air Force archives. The files are not classified but the building is, with the interesting result that one needs a security clearance in order to see these "unclassified" papers. And what about the files of the Condon Committee? One would think that they belonged to the scientific fraternity. Not so. When the project wrote its report the files were locked up by the university. I am told that they were later transferred to a private home, and were burned shortly thereafter.

The Second Coverup

The little town of Carteret lies on the western coast of Normandy, about twenty miles away from Cherbourg. It is situated directly to the north of wonderful Mont-Saint-Michel, a monastery that, as everyone knows, the devil built. On December 2, 1973, a very strange thing happened on the beach at Carteret. Two fishermen, Mr. G. Jean, 44, and his son Noel, 18, got up at 5 A.M. to retrieve their nets at low tide. When they arrived on the beach half an hour later, they saw a very bright object directly over the area where their nets had been spread. They walked toward it until they estimated they were a hundred and fifty yards away, and it appeared as an intense yellow "window," eight feet long and five feet high, emitting a cone-like beam directed toward the ground. The two fishermen were afraid and decided not to get closer. They tried to work without thinking about the object, but then it changed suddenly: the yellow light was turned off. Over the area where it had been hovering there was now a blue-green "football" that flew away at 6:05 A.M.[1]

1. In the celebrated sighting in Pascagoula, Mississippi, which took place on October 11, 1973, and which involved three creatures "floating"

My wife and I investigated this sighting during a research trip through the west of France in December 1973. She went to Carteret less than ten days after the occurrence and spoke to one of the witnesses and to the police investigators while I was checking other information. Many strange data came to the surface. First we found that this was not the first sighting. Two months earlier, the young man had seen three yellow spheres in staggered formation over the same beach while driving with his brother-in-law. The sighting took place about 7 P.M. and the spheres appeared to be about twelve to fifteen feet above ground (rather than "landed on the beach," as reported in *France-Soir*).

"What was the pattern of the lights?" we asked Noel Jean.

"There was a first yellow light, a second one above, a third one to the left above again, and some metal in between."

"What was it doing?"

"The lights came on and off and it followed the car."

"And you, what did you do?"

"We stopped to look at it, and when we got back into the car the lights were turned off on the object."

Since the second sighting the elder man has decided *not to go out of his house anymore.* He no longer goes fishing. He locks himself in his room when the investigators come to ask him questions. Does he know something he does not want to discuss?

We saw no traces on the beach. The gendarmes confirmed to us that the grass in the dunes had not been af-

out of a hovering UFO, the witnesses were again two fishermen: Charles Hickson, 42, and Calvin Parker, 19. During the night of November 6, Rayme Ryan, 42, and his son Larry, 17, as well as Rayme's twin brother Raymond and his son Earl, 16, saw a submerged object in the oyster bed area to the southwest of Pascagoula. In all three of these cases, within two months, there had been fishermen, either an older man and a young one or a father and his son. It is also noteworthy that the Pascagoula fisherman is convinced that "it will happen again." This, too, is a common remark.

fected. There was some barbed wire nearby. It was
checked for magnetic effects. The test was negative. We
heard that a local radio amateur had noticed something at
the time of the near landing and checked the story: his
receiver had been blocked out for several minutes.

"It was in the middle of the nets," Mr. Noel Jean told
us.

"The papers have said that it measured 1.50 by 1.50 meters," we informed him.

"That's not true. It was rectangular, about 2.50 by 1.50
meters. It was as big as a stove [*sic*]!"

"What time did it end?"

"We got there at 5:30. It disappeared between 5:50 and
5:55."

"What happened when the object disappeared?"

"We went away looking at the rectangular light all the
time, and it turned toward the dunes, then came back on
us. It was turned off and then we saw a small blue-green
ball above the spot. It got smaller and after six we couldn't
see anything anymore."

"How big was the ball?"

"It was like a soccer ball."

"What did you do when you got on the beach and saw
the rectangle of light?"

"I started going toward it, but it got brighter and
brighter. So my father said: 'Forget it, come back to this
side.' "

There is a large radar installation near Cherbourg, at a
place called Mauperthuis, located thirty-eight kilometers
away from Carteret. The range of the antenna is two
hundred kilometers. At 6:10 A.M. on that particular morning it picked up an echo in the southwest, moving to the
north of Cherbourg. An object flying from the direction of
Carteret toward Great Britain would have followed this
course. The same morning something peculiar happened
on the coast. The French trawler *Archipel*, which was

close to the rocky coast of Urville, directly west of Cherbourg (on the trajectory the object must have followed if the radar echo corresponds to the UFO) went off course; in view of the frequently observed magnetic perturbations in the vicinity of a UFO, it can be hypothesized that its magnetic navigation system gave erroneous indications. The boat got too close to the coast, hit the rocks and sank, fortunately without loss of life.

The observation of the yellow "window" on the beach had lasted no less than five minutes. Why had the two fishermen not walked closer to the object to ascertain its nature? There seem to be two reasons for this. First, the "window" became brighter as they walked within one hundred fifty yards, and this discouraged them from approaching any closer. And they felt "paralyzed with fear." Whether this "paralysis" was an actual physiological inhibition or the result of psychological fear—or both—has not been ascertained. "A Strange Affair" was the title of the article on the sighting in the tabloid *Minute* the following week.

The observation had taken place early Sunday morning. The following Friday, local people discovered some interesting items on a nearby beach. These consisted of a complete professional set of underwater exploration equipment, a radioactivity tester, sonic signalers, along with trousers and jackets with English-language writing.

Now the local police, with the assistance of the DST (French counter-intelligence) and the SDECE (the organization that constitutes the main intelligence arm of the French government), have discovered that it was a case of underwater radiation detection. Such was the substance of the carefully designed rumor that began circulating.

This is what I call the Second Coverup: the release of official "explanations" that do not explain anything but which provide skeptics with an excuse for dismissing the story. Difficult cases will be swept under the rug at all cost if psychological pressure on the witness is not enough to discourage him from telling his story in the first place.

How could the discovery of some diving equipment "on a nearby beach" explain the two observations of the unidentified objects? What about the radar echo? The "explanation" is completely invalid, but it is typical of stories that are engineered to discredit the witnesses and reassure local populations. These objectives are generally reached. The witnesses are intimidated, and the local police, the only source of accurate data, are generally anxious to see things return to normal.

We were fortunate to be able to investigate this case within a few days of the events, before the coverup was organized. What would be the reaction of a scientist stumbling upon such a case a few weeks or a few months later? He would simply brush it aside, and with good reason. The witnesses are uncooperative; one of them stays home and will not talk to visitors; the local police no longer have anything to say; the military radar operators in Cherbourg have received orders to deny their statements of the night in question; and the information that appears in the newspapers is confused, garbled, and inaccurate.

A local newspaper published a cartoon showing the little town of Carteret, with a flying saucer and a Martian in the foreground. A smiling Frenchman has approached the little Martian and asks: "What kind of mileage do you get?"

In a later development, which will appear ironic in light of the coverup attempts at Carteret, a Cabinet member acknowledged for the first time the reality of the UFO problem as a subject fit for scientific research. In March, 1974, the French Minister of Defense, Mr. Robert Galley, agreed to participate in a series of radio interviews that included reports from witnesses and statements by three French scientists who had studied the UFO phenomenon for many years: Dr. Pierre Guerin, of the Paris Astrophysical Institute; Dr. Claude Poher (head of scientific studies for the French equivalent of NASA); and myself. What the Defense Minister told reporter Jean-Claude Bourret [2] might be a lesson for other government officials around the world:

> I am deeply convinced that we must regard these phenomena with an attitude of completely open mind. A number of breakthroughs have been made in the history of mankind because someone has attempted to explain the unexplainable. Now, among these aerial phenomena that have been gathered under the label of UFOs, it is undeniable that there are facts that are unexplained or badly explained.
>
> In 1954 the Defense Ministry created a special section for the gathering and study of witness accounts regarding these unidentified flying objects. I have before me a number of these accounts, that have developed over the years until 1970; there are approximately fifty of them. Among the earliest ones is a statement of personal observation by Lieutenant d'Emery, Jean, from Air Force Base 107 at Villacoublay, dated November 20, 1953. There are also reports from the Gendarmerie and some observations from pilots and Air Center commanders. There are many elements, whose convergence is of concern, during the year 1954. Therefore the attitude one must have is that of a completely open mind, an attitude in which one does not deny the observations *a priori*. Our ancestors, in prior centuries, must have denied the reality of a number of things that seem to us today absolutely elementary, like piezoelectricity, or static electricity, not to mention biological phenomena.
>
> In fact, the entire development of science consists in the fact that, at a given time, we realize that for fifty years we have had mistaken ideas about the reality of certain phenomena.

It is difficult to add anything to this statement. It is not clear that the simple fact of keeping an open mind about

2. Jean-Claude Bourret, a leading French journalist, has published his investigations and interviews in an excellent book entitled *La Nouvelle Vague des Soucoupes Volantes* (Paris: France-Empire, 1974).

UFOs will in itself make a breakthrough possible but science should certainly welcome the lifting of the attitude that has prevented it from examining the facts.

The Third Coverup

We have so far discussed two forms of coverup: (1) the fact that pressure is placed on witnesses to discourage them from telling their story; and (2) the fabrication of "explanations" when a witness does speak. I believe that to these factors we must add a third one: *the built-in silencing mechanism of the phenomenon itself.*

On December 3, 1967, a patrolman named Herb Schirmer, of Ashland, Nebraska, had an experience that deserves to be placed in the context of the stories of the abduction of Betty and Barney Hill and of the Pascagoula fishermen. At 2:30 in the morning Schirmer saw on the road an object with a row of flickering lights. Believing it to be a truck, he turned on his high beams. The object took off. The 22-year-old patrolman drove back to the station and wrote his entry: "Saw a flying saucer at the junction of highways 6 and 63. Believe it or not."

Schirmer went home with a strong headache and a buzzing noise that prevented him from sleeping. He also had a red welt *below the left ear.*[3] The case came to the attention of the Colorado Committee and Schirmer was placed under hypnosis. It then became clear that there was a twenty-minute period during which he remembered nothing. Later, at the suggestion of another researcher, he was again placed under hypnosis revealing an extraordinary sequence of events.

As he saw the object take off, the patrolman decided to follow it, and drove up a dirt road toward the intense light.

3. In the case of the engineer mentioned in the Introduction a vibration was also reported to have generated pain "under the ear, at the base of the skull." The physiological implications of this consistent observation are interesting: in both cases, the witness might have been hit by the beam of a device to alter his state of consciousness.

He tried to call the police at Wahoo (Nebraska) but the radio was not working and the car engine died. The object, metallic and football-shaped, was surrounded by a silvery glow. It was making a "whooshing" sound, and the lights were flickering rapidly. Legs appeared under the craft, and it landed. Schirmer wanted to drive home, but he was *"prevented by something in his mind"*. The occupants of the craft came toward the car. He was unable to draw his revolver. They shot some greenish gas toward the car, pulled a small object from a holster, flashed a bright light at him, and he passed out!

The next thing Schirmer remembered, under hypnosis, was rolling down the car window and talking to the occupant of the craft, who pressed against the side of his neck and asked him: "Are you the watchman over this place?" then pointed to the power plant and said, "Is this the only source of power you have?"

Schirmer was taken aboard. He saw control panels and computer-like machines. The occupants were wearing coveralls with an emblem of winged serpent. One of them pushed a button and tapes started running. "Through my mind . . . somehow . . . he is telling me things. . . . My mind hurts. . . ."

Remember that my friend the engineer had also seen a machine with tapes but he had spent eighteen earth days facing it.

The occupants gave Schirmer a lot of interesting but possibly misleading information. They wanted him to believe that they came from a nearby galaxy. They had bases in the United States. Their craft was operated by reverse electromagnetism. Their ships had been knocked out of the air by radar, by ionization. They drew power from large water reservoirs.

> They have no pattern for contacting people. It is by pure chance so the government cannot determine any patterns about them. There will be a lot more contacts.

TO A CERTAIN EXTENT THEY WANT TO PUZ-
ZLE PEOPLE.
They know they are being seen too frequently and
they are trying to confuse the public's mind.

Finally the occupant told Schirmer that he was not to remember the inside of the ship. He concluded:

YOU WILL NOT SPEAK WISELY ABOUT THIS
NIGHT. WE WILL RETURN TO SEE YOU TWO
MORE TIMES

And at one point, in a hauntingly beautiful moment, one
of the men took Schirmer to the large window of the ship,
pointed to the deserted landscape around them and said
gravely: "Watchman, some day you will see the Universe!" If the "occupants" are so advanced, and do not
want Schirmer to speak wisely of that night, why could he
remember so much of it under hypnosis? Have they not
anticipated this method of disclosure? Or could it be that
some parts of the human mind are inaccessible to them?
Could it be that their power is more limited than their actions seem to imply? Could it be that someone, or something, is playing a fantastic trick on us?

The Phenomenon Negates Itself

Perhaps you have had the opportunity to attend a magic
show performed by an excellent master of that remarkable
profession. He produces before you, under impossible
conditions, a phenomenon that is clearly unexplainable.
But then he appears to realize how disappointed the audience is. Indeed, everyone feels almost insulted by the pre-
posterousness of his performance. There must be a simple
explanation, an obvious trick! You do not find it . . . then
the magician *explains everything:* the table top was hollow, the cane was made of small sliding sections that he
could collapse into a different shape. Now you have un-

derstood everything, you laugh at yourself for not immediately perceiving such a simple solution. You leave the room with a warm feeling of gratefulness and a certain amount of pride. Yes, pride: "I am not so stupid after all. This little performer hasn't had me fooled for long!"

As you get home, doubts begin to creep into your rational mind. You obtain all the objects necessary for accomplishing the same trick by the simple method so nicely laid bare before you just an hour earlier: and then you realize that the *explanation* itself is impossible, that the magician never told you the real technique!

The UFO phenomenon enjoys the same recursive unsolvability. It leaves indices behind, but they seem to be even more maddeningly misleading than the witnesses' accounts. *The phenomenon negates itself.* It issues statements and demonstrates principles where some of the information conveyed is true and some is false. Determining which is the true half is left as an exercise to the investigator, but the logic is such that one is tempted to place it completely beyond the rational realm: a dangerous temptation!

In some cases all three factors are gathered around a single person, and then the complexity of the research becomes truly fantastic. Uri Geller, of course, is a case in point.

In another relevant case the main witness was fooled by sociologists; the believers were fooled by alleged spacemen calling themselves the "Guardians"; the public was fooled by the believers; and the sociologists may have been fooled by the phenomenon itself!

Contact with a group called the Guardians started when a Midwestern woman referred to as Mrs. Keech woke up one winter morning with a tingling or numbness in her arm:

> My whole arm felt warm right up to the shoulder. . . . I
> had the feeling that someone was trying to get my atten-

tion. Without knowing why, I picked up a pencil and a pad that were lying on the table near my bed. My hand began to write in another handwriting.

Through the messages she got, this woman was gradually introduced into something she regarded as the realms of the life beyond, until one day she received a message of comfort from an "Elder Brother":

> I am always with you. The cares of the day cannot touch you. We will teach them that seek and are ready to follow in the light. I will take care of the details. Trust in us. Be patient and learn, for we are there preparing the work for you as a connoiter. That is an earthly liaison duty before I come. That will be soon.[4]

Mrs. Keech came to think of this as genuine contact with higher entities and began indicating to people around her that new knowledge was coming through. Soon a small sect formed in the Midwestern city where she lived. One of the leaders of the sect was a "Dr. Armstrong," a man we will again find involved in the Uri Geller affair. The Guardians gave the group teachings and advice. They also predicted future events, such as the landings of flying saucers and visits from spacemen. One of these predictions was of a spacecraft landing at a nearby military airfield. The small group drove to a spot from which they could see the runways and observed the scene and the sky in vain, but suddenly a man approached the party, and upon looking at him all present felt an eerie reaction to his appearance. No one had seen him approaching. He was offered something to drink and declined. He walked with a curious, rigid bearing. A moment later he was gone, but no one had seen him go away! As such stories began circulating the belief structure of the little sect became better established. It accumulated its own folklore and even

4. Leon Festinger, Henry Riecken and Stanley Schachter, *When Prophecy Fails* (New York: Harper & Row, 1964).

created its own vocabulary—special words with special meanings.

Mrs. Keech was now writing as much as fourteen hours a day; the teachings became increasingly concerned with religious matters, with cosmology, and with flying saucers. Finally one day the great message came through. It was forecasting a disaster, an earthquake and a flood, and the saving of the believers by their Space Brothers:

> . . . the region of the Canada, Great Lakes and the Mississippi, to the Gulf of Mexico, into the Central America will be as changed. The great tilting of the land of the U.S. to the East will throw up mountains along the Central States.

The group now felt a special responsibility to tell the world about these momentous events. They issued press releases, some of which were picked up by local papers. This in turn attracted the attention of a team of sociologists at the University of Minnesota who were investigating the behavior of individuals in social movements based on specific prophecies. They obtained a Ford Foundation grant to study Mrs. Keech's group and received logistical support from the University's Laboratory for Research in Social Relations. They began infiltrating the sect, pretending to be sincere converts and attending meetings to monitor the evolution of its beliefs as the appointed time for the fulfillment of the prophecy drew nearer.

Although the use of such deception methods by scientists is now very much under question, the book, *When Prophecy Fails,* written by the sociologists on the basis of their investigations, is essential for anyone trying to understand the complex nature of the belief in UFOs. The book details the efforts made by members of the sect to warn mankind of impending doom and describes their belief that those who would be drowned would be spiritually reborn on other planets appropriate to their spiritual development, but that flying saucers would come down from the sky in time to save the believers from the Flood. The predicted events, as the reader must be aware, did not come to pass. The Midwestern part of the U.S. has not been engulfed by the ocean, and the many countries slated for destruction are still above sea level. What did this mean for the beliefs of the sect? *It actually served to reinforce their conviction,* because they took credit for the avoidance of the destruction! Some earthquakes did take place in desert areas around the date of the cataclysm, and had they struck a populated area the damage would have been considerable. Hence, it may have been the light shed by the small group of faithful believers that had spared the country from disaster, they speculated. Some members of the sect also theorized that it had been another test of their ability to believe blindly, to follow without discussion the orders they received from their Guardians, and to face ridicule without fear.

Why bring the story of Mrs. Keech into the discussion of a scientific study of UFOs? Many sociologists will argue that her case is typical of many small sects and cults and that adequate theories now exist to explain their behavior. To a very great extent this is true, but I am not convinced that the mechanism that gives rise to the founding of such movements is fully understood, and I do not believe that their potential impact on society has been made completely explicit.

The case of Mrs. Keech is important to all scientists who have an interest in the UFO phenomenon, because it provides a prototype for an increasing number of groups that establish themselves around similar belief systems. One of the most publicized of these groups in recent years is the network of Uri Geller devotees, which has succeeded in arousing the interest of several leading physicists. In Geller's case, like Mrs. Keech's, there are several unexplained phenomena that provide a basis for the beliefs of the group. In both cases, too, we are told to expect "higher" knowledge to come from the UFOs. And in both cases there is an impact on the collective consciousness.

What about the prophetic element? Mrs. Keech predicted a flood and salvation from above. Geller and Puharich have forecast massive flying saucer landings. Many people around the country (whom author John Keel has appropriately called "the silent contactees") are keeping to themselves what they regard as revelations made to them by alien entities. Perhaps people have always had such experiences. Perhaps they were purely religious, hence private, in times past, and only the relative acceptance of modern UFO sightings by a segment of the media and by a few curious scientists has encouraged the partial disclosure of some of the contacts. Whatever the case may be, we tend to discount too easily the fact that the phenomena contain absurd elements. This is the third coverup.

It is tempting to place Mrs. Keech and all people like her into a category neatly labeled in sociological terms, like "doomsday believers" and "cognitive dissonance," preferably with the magic term "behavior" tacked on. Examining the details of her story, should, however, make us a bit cautious. There is, for example, the matter of the strange man she met in the first prophetic instance. The academic investigators felt that they were on such strong theoretical ground that they neglected to ascertain whether the mysterious appearance and disappearance of the stiff-legged entity could be confirmed by others. This lack of followup must be deplored. On two other occasions, Mrs. Keech had been visited by strange people. The first incident followed the disclosure of her flood forecast in the local papers. Two men came to her door and asked to talk to her; one of them was a perfectly ordinary human, but his companion was very strange and did not say a single word during the visit. She asked who they were, and the first man replied, "I am of this planet, but he is not." The point of their discussion, which lasted for half an hour, was that *she should not publicize her information beyond what she had already done.* "The time is not right now," the man said before leaving with his companion. This encounter had been deadly serious. As a result Mrs. Keech gave up her plans to publish a book about her experiences.

There was another visit, a few months later, this time by five young visitors who spent two hours trying to convince Mrs. Keech and a scientist who was a member of her group that their information was incorrect, that everything they were predicting was wrong.

The investigators again made no effort to identify these visitors, which is in my opinion a serious oversight: "Why these young men called at the house, what their purpose was, and who they were—these are things we do not know: they may have been practical jokers, or they may have had a serious purpose." In describing her discussion with the later visitors, Mrs. Keech said, shocked and weeping, that:

> They kept forcing me to take back things. He kept trying to pressure me into saying they were not true. They kept telling me that what I said was all false and mixed up. And they told me that they were in contact with outer space too and all the writings I had were wrong and that everything I was predicting was wrong.

Now the ring of absurdity was complete around Mrs. Keech. She was experiencing the third coverup. The Flood would not take place. The believers who had trusted all the signs and the obvious sincerity of their medium or "channel" would be left completely isolated—having lost or resigned their jobs, in some cases having sold all their earthly possessions, committed to a reality that only they could perceive; they would be forever unable to tell the whole story. The most highly educated man in the group, a local professor, would comment:

I've had to go a long way. I've given up just about everything. I've cut every tie. I've burned every bridge. I've
turned my back on the world. I can't afford to doubt. I
have to believe. And there isn't any other truth. . . .
You're having your period of doubt now, but hang on,
boy, hang on. This is a tough time but we know that the
boys upstairs are taking care of us.

A frightening view, perhaps one that will in the future
take new forms and engulf more people. Such is the result
of the three coverups.

CHAPTER THREE

Memorandum for Archives

—Are Catholics the Chosen People?
—No. Signed AFFA.
—Can we see a spaceship or flying saucer?
—When would you like to see it?
—Can we see it now?
—Go to the window!

—Exchange between three intelligence
officers and the alleged space
intelligence AFFA, July 6, 1959,
in Washington, D.C., from a Project
Blue Book memorandum

The Contact with SPECTRA

The series of contacts between a physician, Andrija Puharich, a graduate of Northwestern University, and the "Intelligence in the Sky" called SPECTRA or Hoova, began on November 30, 1971, when Puharich hypnotized Uri Geller for the first time. Uri said under hypnosis that he found himself in a cave in Cyprus and "came there for learning."

"I learn and learn, but I don't know who is doing the teaching."
"What are you learning?"
"It is . . . about people who come from space. But I am not to talk about these thing yet." [1]

1. Andrija Puharich, *Uri* (New York: Doubleday, 1974), p. 94.

During this hypnotic session, Geller recalled his early experiences with UFOs as a child. At the age of three, as he was playing in a garden in Tel Aviv, he saw a large shining bowl-shaped light in the sky above him, on December 25, 1949. And there was a huge, very bright shining figure in the garden:

> The shining figure had no face that could be seen, only a radiant countenance. Uri gazed at this radiance in total hypnotism. Then he became aware of arms slowly moving out from the side of the body of the radiance. The arms were raised over the "head" of the radiance, and then Uri saw that held between the hands was the sun. It was so blazing in its brightness that Uri passed out from the power of its rays, with the pain of blindness.

At that point of the hypnotic session, a voice was heard in the room. It identified itself as the source that had found Uri in the garden and had "programmed" him. The message was impressive but also absurd: "We reveal ourselves because . . . plans for war have been made by Egypt." The alleged cosmic intelligence was expressing the same concern that was in the minds of the people gathered in that apartment in Israel, and these people were so overwhelmed by the communication that it did not occur to them that such a cosmic power, if real, would have been able to stop a war with considerable ease. After all, if they can stop automobile engines, why not simply freeze the motions of all the tanks in the Middle East? Instead, Uri and Puharich took the message literally. And they took literally every one of the messages that followed, reading infinite wisdom into pseudoscientific mumbo-jumbo that often emerged from their tape recorder: "There is a dematerialized aspect to your atoms that we can use" (p. 166), and "We need that mass landing like you people on earth call refueling, and charging up, like a huge plane of yours charges up with electricity. We do that through your barometric and cosmic layer around earth" (p. 179). On another occasion, the alleged cosmic intelligence even uttered this piece of wisdom:

> We have passed our souls, bodies and minds into computors [sic] and moved several of millions of light-years backwards toward your time and dimension. In due time we shall receive all material coming back to our main center which is zoned into a different dimension than yours. This different dimension lies beyond the so-called star, and so-called god, so-called planet that you call the sun. It is millions of light-years backwards into the dieshold [?] of the ages.

Not only have Puharich and Geller taken these philosophical and pseudoscientific messages seriously, but they have followed to the letter, with the most extreme reverence, the instructions they received from this alleged cosmic source. The first contact that Puharich had with alleged UFO entities was through the same man who was a leader in Mrs. Keech's sect! (The sociologists who wrote *When Prophecy Fails* called him Dr. Armstrong.) Now, the cases we have already reviewed have prepared us to deal with the material presented by Uri Geller. In this respect I will attempt to convey my feeling of uneasiness about the authenticity of the messages and the intentions of their source.

I have met Dr. Puharich, whom I regard as an intensely sincere man, and I think highly of Geller's talents. We cannot brush aside their experiences, and the experiences of many people who have been close to them, with simple rejections. What we can and should do is to sort out the implications of the extremely confusing set of events they claim to have observed. Here again, as in the Aveyron case, we touch the very essence of prophecy. SPECTRA tells Puharich, at one point, "It is a shame that for such a brilliant mind we cannot contact you directly. Maybe in time we shall be able to contact you directly." Earlier, SPECTRA had said, "Our computers studied everyone on earth. You were noticed for your abilities as the perfect man for this mission." Why would a cosmic intelligence capable of manipulating time and space at will and of controlling the minds of men, use such a primitive device as a computer to sort out the abilities of the earth's population?

But we are not asked to comprehend here; we are asked simply to believe. *We are asked to suspend our rational judgment and to trust the "higher" power that expresses itself through a few chosen people.* This is not new. There is a precedent, too, for a young man from Israel who believes he will save the world. What happens if we refuse to be drawn into blind belief of this sort? What happens if we analyze and compare? We find that the messages from SPECTRA *do not explain UFOs.* They fail to give a consistent interpretation of the characteristics of the sightings in the last twenty-five years; furthermore, we find that the cult that is building up around Puharich and Geller is very similar to a number of other belief structures that have developed in the U.S. and other countries in recent years.

Uri and Puharich receive messages from SPECTRA, predicting mass landings (perhaps visible only to themselves). In the discussions I have had with them they have ignored the fact that similar predictions have been made to others all over the world, allegedly coming from other cosmic sources, each one presenting a consistent philosophy, each one telling obvious falsehoods and uttering sheer jargon most of the time.

The members of the Invisible College have become interested in these patterns, but they have carefully reserved judgment on their nature. We could reject the Geller phenomenon as an aberration or a hoax, and this will be, I suppose, the reaction of many scientists. My own approach is to recognize precisely in what respects it does not resemble what we already know of the UFO phenomenon, and then to place it alongside other, possibly similar problems which have been around for some time. Periodically I try to revise my own prejudices about these unexplained facts and to perceive some pattern that might be a clue to their nature.

The Way to Enlightenment?

Throughout history the minds of men have been manipulated by sources apparently external to their environment. It has been a common theme in all these communications that the purpose of the message was to show mankind a way to enlightenment, to greater happiness, and to salvation, either from physical disasters or from dangers waiting for us beyond death itself. Another common premise in all such inspirational messages was that they originated with "higher" beings, superior to humanity in technology and in wisdom. The historical importance of such communications has generally been trivial but occasionally it has been profound. It has often resulted in the creation of small groups of priests or initiates who claimed direct contact with the higher entities or gods. One of the points of Puharich's book is to place a similar claim before us. For he and Geller are clearly designated as the interpreters of the voice of SPECTRA: "I believe," states Dr. Puharich (p. 127), "that a Prophet, a Uri Geller . . . is specifically created to serve as an intermediary between a 'divine' intelligence and man." In another communication Dr. Puharich was told: "In the last twenty-four hours you have passed the test successfully. This is the last time ever in your life that you will have to be tested. . . . You must tell the world everything about us. . . ." Finally, Dr. Puharich states flatly that "The relationship . . . between these superior beings and Uri and me continues to grow deeper and mutually more meaningful." In other words, Puharich and Uri are initiates, modern-day prophets.

Although most of the messages from SPECTRA are said to have come on a tape recorder, Uri Geller himself has begun to get information through automatic writing. It comes in the form of tensor equations, a kind of higher

mathematics of which Uri has no concept. Puharich and
Geller have failed to note that similar "messages" have
been reported by all sorts of individuals under a variety of
circumstances and that again, most of them have been misleading. There is much to learn from a study of this strange
form of "communication," as some intelligence organizations discovered in 1959.

The Contact with AFFA

The date was July 6, 1959, and the place, Washington,
D.C. I believe the facts to be authentic, and I am sorry that
I must disguise the names of the principals.[2]

On the day in question a gentleman I shall call Mr. Talman, had an experience that caused him to contact Colonel
Friend, then head of Project Blue Book, concerning Talman's personal experiences with psychic phenomena in
connection with UFOs.

Talman and Friend met three days later in the presence
of six men from the Central Intelligence Agency and a rep-
resentative of the office of Naval Intelligence, and they
went over the entire case. The discussion began with a
briefing about official government involvement in the
study of UFOs. Several local cases were studied, as well as
some highly publicized American sightings where photographic evidence had been obtained, especially the
Mariana case of August, 1950, and the Tremonton sighting
of July, 1952. It seems that several members of the group
had had contact with a unit that examined the pictures.

Such evidence, interesting as it was to the participants,
was not the main point of the meeting, and Talman finally
described his own experience. For the last five years his
organization had been studying a woman, Mrs. Swan, who

2. This document has been quoted extensively in the recent book by
Robert Emenegger: *UFOs, Past, Present and Future,* with the permission
of the institutions involved. Thus the facts contained in the memorandum
can now be discussed publicly.

claimed to be in psychic contact with space entities. And one of the investigators, an intelligence officer named Curtis, had learned her technique and had acquired her ability to receive messages from outer space!

The method that Mrs. Swan used in her communications was a simple one. Asking specific questions, she would relax her body completely and, holding a pencil, would await an answer. An "unknown force" would then take control of her arm and write down the reply. Her abilities had been studied in depth by the Canadians, and the U.S. armed forces also had a complete file on her. At that point of his summary, Talman gave the floor to his colleague, Commander Curtis.

Curtis began his statement before the group with the revelation that during the second half of June, 1959, he had indeed flown with another officer to visit Mrs. Swan. The aim of the visit was to observe the contact and to ask a number of questions through this "channel." The meeting took place as planned, and at the end of the session Mrs. Swan suggested that the commander try to make contact with the entities himself. Curtis made the attempt but was unsuccessful.

Upon his return to Washington Commander Curtis had discussed the case with Talman and another colleague and, at their repeated suggestion, tried to contact the entities again. This time Curtis appeared to be successful in receiving messages from a source identified as AFFA living on the planet Uranus.

Curtis was told to write down the questions as they were posed by Talman and another individual. He did this by relaxing his arm completely, allowing it to be controlled, as he described it, by the "outside force" which was responsible for writing the answers. He observed that he was the object of a very intense physical tension during the message transmission.

Some examples of the exchange between AFFA and these three men are as follows:

"Do you favor a particular Government, religion, group or race?"

"No. Signed AFFA."

"Will there be a third world war?"

"No. Signed AFFA."

"Are Catholics the Chosen People?"

"No. Signed AFFA."

"Can we see a spaceship or flying saucer?"

"When would you like to see it?

"Can we see it now?"

"Go to the window."

At that point, the three men rushed to the window but saw nothing. Coming back to the table, Curtis asked, "Are we looking in the right direction?" The response from AFFA did not come through his arm but as a word that Curtis pronounced verbally: "Yes!"

It was 2 P.M. on that day, July 6, 1959, when the three men saw the disk-shaped object. It flew over Washington and was described as having clear edges and a dark center. They called the radar center and were told that, for an unknown reason, the radar return was blocked in the sector they indicated! One of the earlier questions to AFFA had elicited a response dealing with the saucers' difficulty in penetrating the earth's radar network undetected.

Universal Association of Planets

When he heard these revelations, Colonel Friend asked Commander Curtis to make another attempt to contact AFFA as he had done three days earlier, but the trial was unsuccessful. He did get a few replies, but they indicated that "the moment was not favorable." AFFA stated, however, that there was no objection to the members of the group attending the meeting.

Mr. Talman and all the people in attendance at the meeting stated for the record that they had known Curtis for many years, and that he had always been competent, quiet, calm, and very conservative. All thought his experi-

ence to be extremely significant, not only because of his
background, but because of the testimony of two other se-
nior officers who had been with him when the flying
saucer had appeared over the building!

The next day Commander Curtis and Colonel Friend
went to the office where the file of the contact case was
kept. The documents contained in that file showed that
Mrs. Swan had been in communication with the following
entities:

     AFFA   from Uranus

     CRILL   from Jupiter

     ALOMAR from Mercury

     PONNAR also from Mercury

     ANKAR   from the constellation Centaurus

What impressed the investigators was the fact that
through these contacts the woman had been able to answer questions that appeared to be beyond her education
and technical knowledge. However, the visitors were disappointed to find only vague descriptions of the propul-
sion mechanism of the mysterious flying saucers. Some of
the statements alluded to the material that was used in
their construction, but nothing specific was revealed.
Curtis indicated that the Canadians had pursued this particular aspect of the question quite deeply.

The documents in that file gave information on the entities that were responsible for the contact. There existed it
seemed, a certain organization called OEEU, meaning
"Universal Association of Planets," and that organization
had a project called EU or EREVZA, which meant
"Earth." [3] Its aim was never specified. In Chapter Four,

3. The document I am quoting from here is a copy of the original memorandum. The spelling of some of the names differs from that given by
Emenegger in his book. For instance, he has OEEV rather than OEEU,
and EUENZA instead of EREVZA.

however, we shall have the opportunity to analyze in detail the fascinating background of a similar organization whose reputation is rapidly spreading in Spain: it is called UMMO and is attempting to influence human affairs.

The memorandum that was written for archiving purposes as a result of this series of meetings concludes with the writer's evaluation of the personal attitudes within the group. The leader of the interaction, it was stated, appeared to be a man with a fine analytic mind. His only motivation in the case was his respect for Curtis. The latter seemed to be a very stable man: "He occupies—or occupied!—a responsible position," the memorandum goes on to say with tongue in cheek. This officer seemed quite embarrassed when he found himself a center of attention during the initial phase of the meeting, but he later relaxed.

Finally, Talman was said to be "a man with both feet firmly on the ground." *"There is no question,"* the author of the memo concluded, *"that the object seen over Washington on that day of July 1959, was a flying saucer."*

The Contact with 7171

In 1972 I began my own investigation into the phenomenon of automatic writing and I had the occasion to observe several lengthy exchanges between one of my subjects and an entity calling itself "7171," who claimed to be connected with UFOs. The subject was a man whose abilities I have personally tested; in successive experiments involving small objects hidden in plastic boxes, this person produced drawings of the targets with considerable accuracy. (Other tests involved the use of a computer in the prediction of the state of a random number generator.) For several years, this person had occasionally felt the urge to write what at first seemed to be meaningless messages. When questions were asked of the "entity" allegedly producing the writing, the messages became more focused, and soon centered on the UFO phenomenon. This person then approached me and agreed that more systematic testing was in order. At the same time we attempted to refine the communication technique and to identify those components of the interaction that might be coming from the channel's own subconscious mind.

The contents of some relevant communications are given below. The point here, once again, is not that such communications might contain any new knowledge, but that, taken in the context of the "contact" with AFFA, they throw some light on the type of phenomena the men in Washington were playing with.

Vallee: Can you experience the future?

Medium: YES.

Vallee: Why are you communicating?

Medium: THE ANSWER TO THIS I DO NOT FULLY KNOW MYSELF. I KNOW ONLY THAT IT IS CONSISTENT WITH THOSE HIGHER THAN I.

Vallee: What are UFOs a symbol of?

Medium: THEY ARE A SYMBOL OF NOTHING IN THE SENSE THAT YOU MEAN. THEY HAVE A VALIDITY INDEPENDENT OF SYMBOLISM.

Vallee: Why are there men like us in UFOs?

Medium: BECAUSE, FOR VERY DEEP REASONS, THE FORM OF MAN IS A UNIVERSAL CONSTANT.

Vallee: Why do they come here?

Medium: TO HARMONIZE THIS WORLD WITH THE REST OF THE UNIVERSE.

Vallee: Who is 7171?

Medium: HE IS ONLY ONE OF THE INFINITE NUMBER OF ENTITIES THROUGH WHICH I MAY SPEAK.

Vallee: Does he have special significance?

Medium: ONLY IN THE SENSE THAT HE WAS
           CHOSEN AT A PARTICULAR TIME FOR
           CONTACT WITH XXX. (medium's name)

Vallee: Can you serve as a channel to an entity that is
           higher than yourself?

Medium: THERE IS NONE HIGHER THAN MY-
           SELF.

Vallee: You lied when you said that you were the
           supreme source of life, then. Earlier you
           mentioned "those higher than I." Can you
           explain this?

Medium: YES. I AM BOTH. THE APPLE IS BORN
           OF THE TREE, BUT IS ALSO THE
           SOURCE OF ALL APPLE TREES.

Vallee: Can you produce physical effects that we can
           recognize (light, sound)?

Medium: WHEN THE TIME IS RIGHT SUCH
           THINGS WILL OCCUR.

How Belief Is Born

On the basis of such communications, should I now jump
to the conclusion that I am now in contact with a source of
immense wisdom? Should I assume, like Dr. Puharich,
that I have the responsibility to reveal to the world the existence of this higher power? Unfortunately, I cannot
regard the above, or any of the other exchanges I have obtained through this and other channels, as a genuine communication with a higher entity. I do not doubt the truthfulness of the man who acted as channel, and whom I am
happy to have as a friend. Neither do I doubt that there
must be, throughout the universe, billions of entities endowed with thought, of which I would expect, on a purely
statistical basis, about half to be lower than man and half
to be higher. Humanity is, after all, the only form of
evolved intelligence we know (we still have much to learn

about dolphins, however) and we should expect to be about average on the scale of intelligence among galactic civilizations. Why should there be anything exceptional about us?

I regard the above dialogue as an instance of communication with a level of consciousness, possibly (but not necessarily) nonhuman. But its nature may be understandable only in terms of a space-time structure more complex than what current physics places at our disposal. As we attempt a definition of this form of consciousness it is useful to keep in mind that aspects of it may be systematically misleading. Its manifestation in the form of statements in our language may be childish or absurd. Its elements may be borrowed entirely from our own brains and reflected upon us (as seems the case in most of the exchanges between Puharich and SPECTRA) or it may present genuinely new data. Experiences involving automatic writing are not a recent development. The techniques themselves are as old as the Old Testament, which was, after all, written through communication with such a "higher source," and it is difficult to deny that the contents of this communication still rule over the lives and conduct of hundreds of millions of human beings. We are not dealing here with a funny bit of stage magic or with an intriguing source of random incidents. We are dealing instead with one of the most fundamental drives of the human race. How can these manifestations have such a deep relationship to collective consciousness? They make possible the appearance and development of mass religious movements, inspiring entire civilizations to war and conquest, submitting them to the will of leaders who may not hesitate to sacrifice millions of lives to create new forms of society conforming to their vision.

There is an uncanny power in words that appear to issue from a superhuman source, and it would be dangerous to assume that *this power cannot still move the world today.* It is manifested around us in the charismatic movement, in hundreds of occult groups of one kind or another, and in many UFO-related writings such as those inspired by SPECTRA, AFFA, and others we will investigate. This material is variously received as a manifestation from God, as a sign of lunacy, or as a dangerous form of social deviance. Most often, the words of the "entity," whether it claims to be of a space origin or to represent some dead person like "Aunt Martha" does nothing more than borrow words and expressions that exist as thoughts, possibly unconsciously, in the minds of the persons who attend the meeting. For this reason, exposure to such phenomena is hazardous to psychic health! [4]

A perceptive reader of Puharich's book will note that the voice of SPECTRA consistently uses concepts that are current in the thoughts of either Uri or the author himself. In particular, it gets confused about astronomical units of measurement in precisely the same manner as Uri Geller does:

"Millions of light-years backwards into the dieshold [?] of the ages," says SPECTRA (p. 185), confusing units of time with units of space. And on another occasion the Rhombus 4-D computer states: "That was planned hundreds, hundreds of light-years ago, Andrija." And SPECTRA also spoke of "many billions of light-years ahead of time." Therefore we should consider the possibility that we are dealing with a phenomenon that uses, or emanates from, the brains of Geller and Puharich.

Before Dr. Puharich gets too deeply into the tensor equations he is getting from this divine source, I suggest that he should spend a little time straightening out the definition of their physical units, because something is drastically wrong with their idea of light-years! A light-year, contrary to what the name seems to imply, is not a unit of time, but a unit of space, namely the distance between two

4. Catholic priests at the end of the nineteenth century discouraged many French families from experimenting with tables that tipped and tapped uncanny messages from Beyond. The facts were undeniable, and the evidence of the phenomena was as good, if not better, than the evidence for flying saucers. In many cases the effects were the same.

points A and B, such that a light signal sent from A reaches B one year later, at the light velocity of 186,000 miles per second. Time obviously cannot be measured in light-years, Einstein or no Einstein. That would be like saying that Uri Geller weighs twenty inches and that it took Puharich 50.7 kilogauss to write his book. The amusing fact here is that Uri makes exactly the same mistake as SPECTRA. During his first interview with scientists from the Stanford Research Institute, Uri explained the concept of SPECTRA's computers guiding his "powers" and said: "You see, they are computers, which were fed millions of light-years in the future."

Here again he is using a light-year as a unit of time. This, of course, raises in our skeptical minds the thought that Uri may be a clever ventriloquist who has been fooling Puharich for years, simulating the voice of SPECTRA. Things are not, however, so simple. Puharich sometimes receives the messages when Uri is away, and it is difficult to believe that even a clever magician would be able to plant loudspeakers in the walls wherever Dr. Puharich goes.

No valid interpretation of the relationship between Uri Geller and his sources of power can be made without a real understanding of the complex phenomena of automatic writing, spiritual contact, and their many variants. In the wake of Uri Geller's fame, a number of people have begun to receive "messages" similar to those issuing from SPECTRA and Rhombus 4-D. Some of these people are scientists, and they are so amazed by the information they claim to obtain through this channel that they are tempted to drop everything else to devote all their time to such a study. I hope that the data given in this book will serve as a note of caution to these scientists.

It is true, in my opinion, that Geller and other "silent contactees" can produce phenomena that are inadequately explained in conventional terms. It is also undeniable that these phenomena do not constitute an end, but a means for convincing both scientists and nonscientists of the opportunity for contact with a "higher" source of information and power. Here lies the danger, because historically, such messages have never revealed anything that was not already known or within the intellectual grasp of man. The fact that Geller writes tensor equations should not surprise us: Puharich is familiar with this form of mathematics, and it has been consistently observed that messages produced by automatic writing could tap the knowledge, conscious or unconscious, of the participants. The following previously unpublished case is an example of this phenomenon: nothing that is within the power of any one of the participants is beyond the power of the alleged entity.

In 1899, the great French astronomer Camille Flammarion, who was also a keen psychic investigator, reported that he had once attended a spirit séance at the home of the poet Victor Hugo, whose wife and brother also attended. There were three other distinguished guests, Messrs. Vacquerie, Guerin, and Allix. They sat around a table and evoked the spirit, who soon responded and identified himself as the ghost of Molière. Everything went fine until someone asked the entity to provide information about the problem of death. Molière was then replaced by another entity, who took over the tapping and answered through the table in a magnificent poem of eight lines:

> Spirit, eager to know the secret of the night
> Holding between your hands the terrestrial light,
> You would come, stealthily, among shadows of gloom,
> Running a searching hook through this enormous tomb!
>
> Go back to your silence, and extinguish your flame,
> Go back into this night out of which you came;
> No living eye eternal books has read
> Over the shoulders of the Dead! [5]

5. The French text that I am here attempting to translate, went much more beautifully, as follows:

> *Esprit qui veut savoir le secret des ténèbres*
> *Et qui, tenant en mains le terrestre flambeau,*

The good faith of the experimenters can hardly be doubted. Flammarion was so shaken that he did not publish this fact, reporting it only in a manuscript letter to Paul Souday, a journalist friend whose advice he was asking in this instance. The intriguing point is that the table was generating, through what must have been an excruciatingly long series of taps, one of the finest pieces of poetry that Victor Hugo could have written! After such a feat on the part of the entity (who signed "The Shadow of the Sepulchre" for good measure!) I do not doubt that through a similar mechanism Uri Geller can sit down in Puharich's presence and cover page after page with Hamiltonian tensors. If a simple table can use the mind of Victor Hugo, and tease him by generating such a poem, why couldn't Geller "borrow" some mathematical symbols from the mind of Puharich? I see nothing here that requires the intervention of an alien agency. I think the phenomena involving the table can be explained by unconscious and mental process among the attending "spiritualists." The same explanation holds true for Puharich and Geller. Whatever force they are contacting in this fashion shows no evidence of being higher than man.

The Story of John Dee

"John Dee and Edward Kelly claim to be mentioned together," writes Charles Mackay, "having so long been associated in the same pursuits, and undergone so many strange vicissitudes in each other's society." [6] One might wonder whether a future historian will not have the same

> Vient furtif à tâtons dans nos ombres funèbres
> Crocheter dans l'immense tombeau!
>
> Rentre dans ton silence et souffle tes chandelles
> Rentre dans cette nuit dont quelquefois tu sors;
> L'oeil vivant ne lit pas les choses éternelles
> Par-dessus l'épaule des morts!

6. Charles Mackay, *Extraordinary Popular Delusions and the Madness of Crowds* (New York: Noonday Press, 1967), p. 170.

thing to say about Dr. Puharich and Uri Geller. Dr. Dee was a brilliant man, born in London in 1527, who entered Cambridge at the age of fifteen. There he began to develop a keen interest in the occult, and found himself under pressure to leave. From England he went to Louvain, in the Low Countries, where he studied with the disciples of that great master in the magic arts, Cornelius Agrippa. He returned to England in 1551 and obtained through some friends a pension from the king, Edward VI. He became an astrologer and enjoyed the favor of Queen Elizabeth, seeking the elixir of life and the philosopher's stone, and generally having a happy life. He served also as an intelligence agent to Elizabeth, and signed his reports from abroad with the now-famous number 007.

One day in November, 1581, Dr. Dee was contacted by an entity. He was working in his museum, whose window faced west, when a dazzling light appeared. In the middle of the light was the form of an entity who introduced itself as Angel Uriel. Dr. Dee was speechless. The angel smiled and gave him an object, a convex crystal, and told him to use it whenever he wished to converse with the beings of another sphere. All he had to do was to gaze into the crystal, where the beings would appear and "unveil to him all the secrets of futurity."

In his use of the crystal, Dr. Dee discovered two facts. First, he had to concentrate all of his awareness into the crystal (which was in fact a black stone, or piece of polished coal, according to an account published in Granger's *Biographical History*) in order to see the beings, and, second, he could never remember his conversations with them, a fact which is not unlike the mysterious disappearance of Dr. Puharich's tapes when he records the voice of SPECTRA.

In order to record the communications, Dr. Dee confided the secret of the stone to his assistant, Edward Kelly. On December 2, 1581, the first of many sessions took place, and the complete text of these communications is now kept among the Harleian manuscripts at the British Museum. Among the facts revealed by the entities with whom Kelly and Dee were in contact, was a complete language known as Enochian, which is still regarded by contemporary occultists as a tool of the greatest power. Aleister Crowley, for instance, expressed his greatest magical invocations in the Enochian language, which has to be pronounced in a certain way in order to be effective, and these are still used today by his many disciples.

What could the adventure of Dr. Dee have to do with UFO's, with SPECTRA, and with the events reviewed in this book? First of all, the fact that the entity appeared, as it did, in dazzling brightness, and delivered the crystal, is certainly of interest here. The fact that Dr. Dee himself was speechless with awe and wonder is also curious. As a trained occultist and magician, Dee must have often experimented with invocations and evocations and could be expected immediately to challenge the intruder with powerful formulas. Instead he remained speechless; also of interest is the fact that a series of messages is presented, whose language is not understandable at first, but must be translated with the help of a linguistic device. We will have occasion to recall this interesting bit of folklore when we discuss the phenomena surrounding the Mormon prophets in later chapters. But the most interesting discovery in the entire episode was made by my friend Donald Hanlon, when he pointed out the fact that the expression AFFA exists as a word in the Enochian language. *The Enochian word AFFA means "empty"!* When the three intelligence officers were being told in 1959 that World War III would not take place, and when they were shown a flying saucer over the capital of their country, they were in direct communication with . . . emptiness!

In the psychic literature there are cases where the entities which manifest themselves by guiding the hand or using the voice of a human channel seem to exhibit a level of knowledge beyond that of the medium; however, such a fact can seldom be proved. The fact that the writing appears much more beautiful than anything the person can produce in a normal state means nothing, as it is often sufficient simply to unlock the unconscious mind to release a veritable stream of artistic energy. To use it productively is another matter, as the adepts of the psychedelic movement have painfully discovered.

I do not mean to imply that genuine psychic phenomena do not take place in automatic writing, or even through that old device of divination, the Ouija board. Communications may be received from a variety of sources—minds of other people perhaps or (who knows?) a higher level of awareness that is attached to no human head. These entities have been known to masquerade as departed souls, as great minds of antiquity, as denizens of other planets. There is no question that some of their statements can achieve dimensions of real beauty and can assume a very prophetic stance.

Shortly after the turn of the century, a cult similar to that of Mrs. Keech flourished in Washington, D.C.[7] It was called the Order of the Initiates of Tibet and was presided over by Miss Marsland, daughter of George Marsland, the founder of the American Bankers' Association. In 1909 the cult had five thousand followers, among them prominent members of the social and diplomatic set. Miss Marsland received her teachings from a mysterious source in Paris. (Allegedly they emanated from Tibet, were written in Sanskrit, and were translated into French by the high initiate in Paris.) The mission of the sect was to "draw men from the study of material effects which has so far occupied the exclusive attention of scientists, and to direct them to the study of cause, force, vibration and the unseen." The resulting advancement would "transmute the scientist into a Magus" and lead to contact with the inhabi-

7. See in particular "Washington's Most Curious Cult—Under the Leadership of a Woman" in the *Washington Post,* October 31, 1909.

tants of other planets. This sect is an interesting precursor
to the various movements and cults that are active today.

In 1966 a woman named Nell Heberling published a
volume of automatic writing entitled *The Golden Message
from Crellritus*. It contained the following, that I find
much more relevant to our present time than the statements of AFFA:

> Your wise men hold their knowledge high,
> Yet fail to see that in your sky
> Truths dwell beyond your feeble minds so small.
> You think that you have grasped it all
> In experiments of great scope;
> Yet bound are you. You dare to hope
> That someday soon you reach beyond your sky
> To *Something* else. Not *other worlds*, this be your cry.
> Not *other races* who may think and hope and fear.
> What, then? Mere planets made of things you hold as
> dear,
> That may be broken down and labelled fast?
> Such fools you be!
> Dream on, the day has not yet come to pass
> When you will face that which you cannot face.

The woman who published these lines warns us in her
introduction: "I did not write this book, I recorded it
only," and she adds, "I have received a large portion of
the second volume, but cannot release it at this time. Too
advanced knowledge can be more dangerous than too little
knowledge." She has left her home town and now is said
to live as a recluse. Those who have seen the second book
tell me that it deals almost entirely with flying saucers.

Before she went away, however, she left these lines:

> The secret lies in those who possess minds, full free,
> But still untaught, know not then what they be. . . .

CHAPTER FOUR

The Function of OEMII

The cast of light you see in the southern sky is of our direction and is pulsating with a turning, spinning motion of the craft . . . which is to land upon the planet in the cast of the day of August first.

—Communication from the Guardians to Mrs. Keech, quoted in *When Prophecy Fails* by Festinger, et al. Received by automatic writing.

In March 1950 a lenticular spacecraft established contact with the Earth's lithosphere for the first time. . . . The descent took place near the village of La Javie, in France. We are a people older than yours, that has reached a level of civilization which is higher too.

—Communication from UMMO to a Spanish writer in 1968. Received in the mail.

SPECTRA is the name of a spacecraft which we use as you use a planet. It has been stationed for the past eight hundred years over the earth. . . . The Israeli territory is where we first landed on earth. . . . We hope to land on your planet in a few years. We are seen more and more by people. We will enter your orbital system through[?] transformation and be able to enter your environment. You may not understand this.

—Communications from SPECTRA to Uri Geller and Andrija Puharich in 1972. Received on magnetic tape. The tape disappeared after transcription.

A Craft with an Insignia

Carlos thought that the weather would soon be too hot for his customary evening walks. But in late spring the air was delightful. He sat on the grass and enjoyed the smell of the pine trees. He opened the paper he had bought at the bus station on his way back from Madrid, and turned to the sports page. All was peaceful for several minutes. Then a child's cry made him look up.

A craft was rising behind a line of trees to the northeast and it followed a curved trajectory toward the power lines. It was a large lens-shaped object, no less than forty meters in diameter. When it suddenly flipped on one side, Carlos lost sight of its brilliant dome. He dropped his newspaper and rose to his feet. He was struck by the strange insignia on the underside of the craft: it resembled a capital H with a vertical bar in the center. It was not quite the astrological symbol for Uranus, and could have passed for a cyrillic letter if the vertical sides had been slightly curved. Others would later describe it as an M, or as an H, but Carlos clearly saw the middle bar.

The formidable craft swung to the right, stabilized, and reached a point to the southeast, where it again veered, exposing its insignia for the second time before turning north. For several minutes it remained stationary near the castle; then it flew up at an unbelievable speed and was lost to the view of all. Its color had gradually turned from bright yellow to orange, and finally to red.

Carlos looked around at the dozens of people who were still staring at the sky, hoping that the craft would come back. There were entire families who had been resting near the pine trees. There were workers with their wives, returning from Madrid. There were children playing. The sun had just set. The date was June 1, 1967. The place was a quiet suburb named San Jose de Valderas. "I wonder what the newspapers will have to say about this," thought Carlos.

The next morning, Mr. Antonio San Antonio, graphics editor of the Madrid evening paper *Informaciones*, received a telephone call from a man who told him he was placing at his disposal five extraordinary photographic documents, the negatives of a series of shots he had been fortunate enough to take at San Jose de Valderas the previous evening. The man declined to give his name. The negatives, he said, could be picked up at a photographic laboratory of Calle General Ricardos. The paper published the five pictures, admittedly very bad ones.

Oddly enough, the negatives were not in sequence. It was assumed that the mysterious photographer had kept a few of the sensational pictures for his private use.

When the testimonies were published and the photos produced, considerable excitement arose in Madrid. Private investigators rushed to the scene and issued calls for additional details.

Two months later, on August 26, 1967, another witness named Antonio Pardo produced two photographs that were as poor as the first series, along with several additional items. Here again, telephone contact was established with the mysterious man, but when investigators tried to meet him he could not be located.

When plotted on a map against the flight of the object, both sets of pictures agreed with the descriptions of its motion. But the two photographers had mysteriously vanished.

A Perfect Case?

A young man in his early thirties who was driving toward the Madrid suburb of Santa Monica between 8:30 and 9:00 that same evening observed an oval glow with a white center and diffused yellow edges going down rapidly towards a restaurant known as La Ponderosa. He then saw the light rise and vanish.

In Santa Monica, at Number 33 Calle de Sedano, lives Mr. Rivero, a shopowner. This gentleman was just going out when he saw a "conical thing" giving off a fiery light, flying over the trees and rising rapidly.

In Apartment 27-B of the Colonia Santa Monica, a large residence that overlooks the Ponderosa area, lives Doña Eugenia Arbiol Alonso. Together with her mother, she observed the same object from her window. In their book *Un Caso Perfecto*, Antonio Ribera and Rafael Farriols give a record of an investigator's conversation with her:

> "Look, there is La Ponderosa."
> "Yes."
> "As you can see, to the left—that is, to the right of La Ponderosa, there are some pine trees, some tall trees."
> "These dark trees?"
> "Yes, those and a bit farther, over there, you understand? Near the trees, where the trucks are going. . . ."
> "Between the trees and the trucks?"
> "Yes, yes, there I saw the thing."
> "On the ground or up in the air?"
> "No, no. I saw it land."
> "Land precisely there?"
> "I saw a thing, as I'm telling you . . . as if it had airplane lights or portholes. And then I saw it was a round thing, as I'm telling you, like a gasoline tank—I imagine that it was round, I didn't think it was flat on the other side. And then, looking at it, I saw it was coming down. 'What a strange thing!' I said to myself. 'The kids must be doing something over there.' . . . and then it landed there, or at least from that distance it gave me the impression that it landed on the ground. Later it rose and stopped a few meters above ground and then it was— Now you see it, now you don't . . . and I cannot say where it went." [1]

Antonio Muñoz is a young man who was inside the restaurant La Ponderosa at the time of the incident. He was standing atop a ladder, placing colored bulbs in preparation for the arrival of the evening customers. A man suddenly rushed in:

"Listen: I was just driving on the road . . . and I saw a

1. Antonio Ribera and Rafael Farriols, *Un Caso Perfecto* (Barcelona: Pomaire, 1969), p. 131.

light that flew horizontally and came down. It was yellow,
at great altitude, but it rapidly got bigger and came down
almost on top of me. I think the craft or whatever it was
has landed right near La Ponderosa."

Antonio Muñoz thought the man was mad, sent him
away and did not bother to investigate.

Five or ten minutes later a couple arrived in a car. The
lady was very nervous, and the man told Muñoz they had
seen a lighted object land two hundred meters away. The
lady started crying. The man, middle-aged, was fairly calm
and drew a sketch of the object that showed a symbol on
its underside, resembling the letter H.

Two young couples arrived next, the girls holding each
other and weeping. A huge sphere of fire, they said, had
come toward them diagonally and had landed near their
car.

The middle-aged man came back later and spoke to
Muñoz again. Later that night he went to the site of the
landing. The next morning, the same man found the three
marks that formed an equilateral triangle six meters in
size. Each trace was a rectangle thirty by fifteen centime-
ters, fairly deep. At the center of the triangle the grass
burned and a metallic powder was found.

There was another visit that same evening. Several men
came to the restaurant and spoke to Muñoz. When he told
them of the witnesses' description they got excited, saying
it corresponded to a signal they had received which was
from another planet. In the following days several of the
shopowners in the area received a curious letter written in
Spanish in a peculiarly formal and ornate style, the un-
dated letter was signed by the French name of Henri
Dagousset. It began:

> Dear Sir:
> On June 1st of this year 1967 took place an incident
> that was mentioned by the press of Spain and by the In-
> formation Agencies of European Countries. In a certain

piece of land situated near km. 3 of the Boadilla del Monte road (Madrid) classified under the heading "Property of the National Estate," has landed an aerial vehicle of round shape that the daily papers have qualified as a "flying saucer."

A few days later, a steel worker and a young girl who resides in the locality of Santa Monica discovered some metallic cylinders with a central disk whose dimensions are provided here for reference purposes: Length of the tube, 129.8 mm. Caliber of the tube, 8.8 mm. Diameter of the central metallic disk, 24 mm. Both capsules are now in our hands and we are enclosing the photograph and drawing of one of them. The outside appearance is that of an aluminum cylinder, with rounded ends.

According to our information, an unknown number of these small cylinders have been found by other residents of the area. Certainly, they can have no value for their present owners (beyond the obvious curiosity that comes from their discovery) and since you own an establishment legally open in that area of the Capital of Spain, we beg you to bring the present communication to the attention of your patrons and neighbors.

We are willing to offer up to 18,000 pesetas [exactly $300] for each one of the cylinders that conform to the enclosed model. In cases where the capsule is found to be deteriorated or broken, as long as the contents are found in good condition we shall study a new offer with the owner.

In recognition of your kindness in giving publicity to the present note (copies of which have also been sent to five other establishments) we shall offer you 7,000 pesetas for each capsule that we secure through your assistance. . . .

A concluding paragraph of the letter indicated the purpose of the investigation:

Our interest is purely scientific. The capsules in question do not contain any device of military interest, but, we repeat, genuinely technical. Our activities are restricted to the study of the so-called U.F.O. (unidentified flying objects) popularly named in this Nation "Platillos Volantes."

Mr. Francisco Arroyo, the manager of a bar called Santa Monica, received a copy of this letter. So did Mr. Muñoz, the owner of La Ponderosa. And according to him, Mr. Rivero, the shopowner quoted above, also received a copy. With the letter came a separate note:

ALL CORRESPONDENCE MUST BE DIRECTED
BEFORE JUNE 28TH TO
Mr. Antoine NANCEY
Lista de Correos—Madrid

Analyzing the Capsules

A Spanish investigator named Farriols was fortunate enough to obtain one of the capsules. It had allegedly been found by a 12-year-old boy who broke it open with a pair of pliers. This important piece of evidence was not directly obtained by Farriols, however. It was given to him by another UFO amateur who had received it from Antonio Pardo—the same man who had produced one of the sets of photographs at San Jose de Valderas—the man who was never interviewed in person by any of the investigators. As someone was later to remark, the name Antonio Pardo can be translated as Anthony Brown.

The device that was examined by Farriols and Ribera contained a piece of green plastic on which the very symbol of the UFO was engraved: three vertical bars crossed horizontally. According to the boy, there had been two pieces in the cylinder, and a peculiar liquid had escaped from it and evaporated when he broke it open.

It so happens that Mr. Farriols' uncle is the president of INTA, the Spanish National Institute for Space Research. The objects were taken into the laboratories of INTA and carefully analyzed. An extensive technical study then revealed the following:

1. The capsule itself was made of nickel of a very high

degree of purity (99%) with traces of magnesium, iron, titanium and cobalt, silicon, and aluminum. (Microphotographs have been obtained and are published in Ribera and Farriols' book.)

2. The plastic material was identified by spectral analysis as polyvinyl fluoride, entry No. 5.29 in the book *Identification and Analysis of Plastics,* by J. Haslam and H. A. Willis.

At the time of the events, this material was made exclusively by duPont de Nemours in the United States, under the brand name of TEDLAR. Its use was restricted and the product was not sold commercially. TEDLAR has an extraordinary resistance to ultraviolet radiation, weathering, dissolvents, chemical agents in general, and abrasion. It is used by NASA at Cape Kennedy to cover rockets on their tower prior to launching. The same material is also noted for "some military applications."

Needless to say, TEDLAR cannot be obtained on the open Spanish market. To confuse matters even further, no one by the name of Henri Dagousset, and no one by the name of Antoine Nancey could be located in Madrid.

The Contact with UMMO

Fernando Sesma Manzano is a Spanish government employee and a minor literary figure in Madrid. In 1954 he founded a UFO group called "Sociedad de Amigos del Espacio." For several years he avidly read the flying saucer literature and hoped that some day he would be contacted by space beings. He was, therefore, well prepared when a man with a strong foreign accent called him on the telephone in the early days of January, 1965, and started uttering a sequence of strange words that Sesma very carefully wrote down.

Speaking in Spanish, the stranger indicated that he was going to forward some items of an "extraterrestrial order."

"Why not meet in person?" Sesma asked.

"This is not possible at the moment. I am under strict orders."

In the following months, Sesma was flooded with typewritten material and telephone calls from his outer-space friends. Information also arrived in the form of letters from as far away as Australia, making reference to events that had taken place in Madrid only some forty-eight hours before. Some of the communications contained wonderful three-dimensional photographs. In hundreds of pages filled with specific technical details as well as philosophical considerations, he saw unfolding the complete system of thought of an alien life form—the race from planet UMMO which was responsible for the flying saucer activities on earth!

Whether they came from Australia, Spain, or some other place, the documents were always stamped with the symbol of the UMMO General Government, three vertical bars crossed horizontally.

On February 6, 1966, in Aluche, a suburb of Madrid not far from San Jose de Valderas and Santa Monica, between 8:00 and 9:00P.M., a large circular object was seen to land by a group of soldiers at a nearby ammunition dump. The object was also seen by Mr. Vicente Ortuno and by a man named José Luis Jordan who was driving toward Madrid. Jordan's account (published in the Barcelona magazine *Porque* of February 16, 1966 and in subsequent articles by Ribera) can be summarized as follows. He saw a whitish disk coming closer to him, its color changing to yellow and orange. Getting out of his car he watched it come down near an airfield. He drove closer, in time to see the disk, about thirty feet in diameter and amazingly luminous, as it rose quickly from the gorund. It was making a steady muted vibration. Suddenly, it just "went out." Three deep rectangular marks were later found at the site.

As the disk flew up, Jordan clearly saw its underside. It bore a peculiar symbol, the insignia of UMMO. To Fernando Sesma and the very few people in Madrid who had in their possession several documents stamped with the same symbol, the coincidence was indeed fascinating.

The Messages

We wish to inform planet Earth of our origin and proceedings and the objectives of our visit to you. We come from UMMO, a planet that revolves around the star IUMMA, recorded on your earth under the denomination Wolf 424.

We received instructions on 12 January, 1965 (Earth Christian Era) regarding the orientation and limits of this information. Approved redaction. . . .

Following some considerations regarding the difficulties of expressing UMMO concepts in Spanish, the document received by Sesma continued:

We proceed, as we have said above, from the planet or solidified celestial body UMMO, whose characteristics we indicate as follows:

Orbit: elliptical with the star Wolf 424 (IUMMA) that serves as our Sun, as focus.

Distance from focus Wolf 424 to the focus of the solar system on January 4, 1953: 3.68502 light-years.

By telephone, Fernando Sesma requested a correction of the latter distance, as it appeared erroneous to him. He was told that the distance was given here as the "true distance," which varied greatly from day to day according to the advanced physical concepts of UMMO. Coming to the solar system along such a route would be like going to Australia by a direct tunnel through the earth.[2]

According to the same series of messages, the mass of

2. The emissaries from UMMO are implying that one can travel through higher dimension much in the way in which a man could go from one point of the surface of the earth to another by leaving it in Spain and re-entering it in Australia.

UMMO is 514 × 1,021 tons and the acceleration of gravity there is 11.88 m/sec². Atmospheric conditions are close to those on earth, so that it is logical to find that the inhabitants of UMMO look very much like us, except that they have no tonsils. Between the ages of 14 and 16 the vocal chords of the children become sclerosed; for this reason, the adult inhabitants of UMMO are unable to express themselves verbally and must use a telepathic function. This is accomplished by holding in one's consciousness the mental image of one's correspondent, and sending impulses of an approximate duration of 0.14 milliseconds. Such impulses are known as "BUAE BIEE." Thanks to a special bilingual code it is possible to employ this technique in double simultaneous conversations.

It is noteworthy that some adults on UMMO keep their normal, earth-like phonetic organ in exception to the rule. This was the case for the messengers who spoke to Sesma by telephone.

The most complete exposition of the nature of UMMO that I have seen is a concise document written in French that originated in West Germany and was written in an awkward style that might betray a Spanish author, although other elements seemed to indicate that the writer found difficulty in using not only French but *any* human language.

> We are well aware of the transcendental nature of this message. We realize that a statement of this nature is usually formulated by a hoaxer, a mentally deranged person with fantastic ideas or, perhaps, by some journalist, some advertising man, or some agent of a political, esoteric or religious organization who might aim at using the version or the information for the benefit of his group.

The letter continued on a cautionary note. The reader was invited to be extremely critical and to take the most painstaking care to ascertain the truth of the statements that followed—statements, it was pointed out, that rested solely on witness' accounts and whose real origin was, after all, unknown to the reader, although, to the authors of the documents, they were clearly evident. When it came to the UFOs, the letter was even more cautious.

> In the last few years, at the occasion of the appearance of the UFO's in the Earth's atmosphere, Man's fantasy has surpassed itself, and one has seen in the press some informations concerning these phenomena that were often fraudulent, rarely authentic.
>
> We are aware that these versions have created an understandable atmosphere of mistrust, and we know that our statements will be necessarily greeted with extreme reservation. However, our aim in sending you this document, typed by one of our assistants, is not to be believed without any evidence more extensive than these few paragraphs.

The document then indicated that "groups of educated persons who know of our existence although, at our suggestion, they keep a discreet silence on the subject, exist in Canada, Austria, Spain and Jugoslavia." It continued with an explanation of the contact with our planet:

> At 05 hours 17 minutes CMT of Earth day March 1950, an OAWOLEA OUEWA (lenticular spacecraft) established contact with the Earth's lithosphere for the first time in our history. The descent took place near the village of "La Javie," in the Basses-Alpes, in France.
>
> We are a people older than yours, that has reached a level of civilization which is higher too. Our social structure is also a different one. We are governed by four members who are selected by psychophysiological evaluation. Laws are regulated as a function of socio-metric constants measured in time.
>
> Our economic system, too, is different. We do not know money, since transactions in such few valuable items as exist on UMMO take place through a network of

what you would call electronic computers. Normal con-
sumer goods are practically impossible to price as their
abundant production greatly exceeds demand.

Our society is deeply religious. We believe in a Cre-
ator (WOA) or God, and we possess scientific arguments
in favor of the existence of a factor that you would call
"soul." We know of a third factor that links it to the body
and is constituted by krypton atoms embedded within
the cephalic mass.

We do not mean to interfere with the social evolution
of your planet for two transcendental reasons. A cosmic
morality forbids any paternalistic attitude on planetary
social networks that must be individually created by
each of them. Furthermore, any public intervention on
our part—our own official presentation, would produce
grave alterations, incalculable social perturbations, and
thus the study and analysis of your Society in its current
virgin conditions would be impossible.

Our modest attempts at contact, such as the one we are
now making with you, will not cause a great change, for
we anticipate the natural skepticism that greets them.

A Mysterious Society

The UMMO affair gained prominence during 1970 and
1971, rapidly becoming the most important subject in the
minds and conversations of European UFO groups. It
would be very wrong to assume, however, that the fascination exerted by the mysterious documents was limited to
such circles. In Spain, high officials in the government, the
law-enforcement agencies, and the military had become
firm believers in the reality of a planet that circled Wolf
424, many light-years away.

In France the situation took a peculiar turn. When the
United States Air Force released the negative conclusions
of the Condon study on UFOs, these conclusions were
prominently displayed in the Paris press. The result, however, was not what the U.S. Air Force had expected. The
French had quietly accumulated their own data on the
subject and, although these files were not available to most

scientists, there was no lack of military personnel and technical experts in France who knew what the real situation was. Some of them had joined UFO research groups in Paris. Others, in high official positions in the French Space Agency, were working alone, secretly.

Through various private channels these scientists heard of the UMMO documents, were provided with copies, and had them translated with great care. They were intrigued by the "rational" approach to the problem of cosmic contact evident in these documents. The background of the Aluche, San Jose de Valderas, and Santa Monica sightings was fascinating.

The UMMO documents are exceptional in two respects: first, they provide a wealth of technical data that the reader is kindly invited to check, and, second, the groups of persons contacted by UMMO are requested NOT to disseminate this information, and, in particular, *not to reveal such communication to their governments.*

Late in 1969 the UMMO documents were already the subject of technical discussions outside Spain. In Argentina, a prominent journalist contacted the La Plata Observatory, near Buenos Aires, and provided the staff with the astronomical parameters concerning UMMO. According to the information he relayed back to Spain, after spending "entire days and nights" studying the figures, these astronomers had reached the conclusion that the planet UMMO must exist. At the occasion of the Twentieth Congress of Astronautics in Mar del Plata, further conversations on the subject took place among a little group whose conclusion was that "in order to shoot down the UMMO theory one needs, astronomically speaking, very strong arguments."

In June, 1971, a three-day meeting of researchers who had become fascinated with UMMO took place in Spain. There were four people from Madrid, all of them close associates of Fernando Sesma. Half a dozen persons came from Barcelona. A professional biologist came from Paris.

This biologist showed extreme interest in the UMMO concept of "biogenetic bases." His presentation before the group included the spectacular announcement that, as soon as he returned to Paris, he would attempt to test the theory that krypton could be found in the human hypothalamus, as stated in some of the UMMO documents.

At the same meeting, several of the UMMO believers contributed nearly fanatical statements on the subject, displaying something that closely resembled religious conviction. (One of them even read an "Ode to UMMO"!)

A Spanish engineer analyzed a certain document concerning the IBOZOO UU, which contains "an exposé of the errors of modern physics." This document was shown to compare favorably with advanced texts written by Minkowski and Eddington. This engineer agreed with the physicists of the French group GEPA, in saying that UMMO physical concepts were absolutely consistent. If these concepts were not of extraterrestrial origin, it was pointed out, then they must have originated with people who knew perfectly the "ultimate advances of modern physics," and had extrapolated beyond them.

The Warning to Mankind

Men of the Earth!

We convey to you our sincere condolences at the occasion of the death of your brother, thinker and mathematician Bertrand Russell.

The expeditionary group that originated with the solidified celestial body UMMO is found among the citizens of various nations on Earth, with the Man Bertrand Russell and others among his brothers: Mirandas K. Gandhi, Ernesto (Che) Guevara, Helder Camara, John XXIII, Martin Luther King, Karl Marx, Emmanuel Mounier, Albert Schweitzer, Tolstoi, and others.

They have dedicated their life to transforming the society into which they were inserted, orienting it in the direction of negative entropy towards forms more in conformity with the ethical norms of collective coexistence.

In another document, treating specifically philosophical, moral, and logical questions, UMMO cautioned the humans it had contacted against falling into the trap of cultism.

> In no way do we wish—and we sternly warn you about this—to see you fall into the temptation of switching your religious, scientific and politico-economical ideas for ours. You will understand yourselves the reason for such a warning. In the first place, the informations we give you are purely descriptive. We present you with an account void of positive arguments, rationales, and proofs supporting them. It would be a mistake for you to adopt our ideas, concepts and statements at face value, within the ideological constellation formed by your teachers on Earth. Besides, if you acted in that fashion, you would alter dangerously the normal rhythm of social existence and the future Culture on Earth. You would modify the normal technological process, damaging the current geosocial balance. A revolution of your structures must take place under the sign of the proper social network. A cosmic morality such as the one we share forbids us to intervene, outside of unpredictable special circumstances.

It is interesting to note that other factors existed in the development of UMMO, factors that were of a more sinister nature than the simple expression of personal exuberance. There was, in the first place, the fact that a military technical school and airfield lies at the focus of the three sightings that provide UMMO with all its "evidence." Then there are the capsules, the strips of TEDLAR.

A military intelligence group could have a number of reasons either to sponsor or stage the UMMO process: the motivation, for example, could be simply a project for training intelligence agents. Was UMMO an exercise in camouflage that got out of hand? If the purpose was the creation of a small nucleus of fanatics, the "exercise" certainly succeeded!

In my opinion, however, UMMO is more than a simple

intelligence exercise. In the previous chapter I mentioned the case of the woman who was in contact with AFFA. She gave information on a certain "Universal Association of Planets" called OEEU, a term which has a certain morphological similarity with UMMO. In both cases, messages are received that are allegedly originating with an extraterrestrial society. One might be tempted to infer that there was a link between the two groups of events.

It would be comforting to discover that the claims in the UMMO stories can be disposed of as mere hoaxes, but such is not the case. In fact, many of the UMMO documents giving details of local conditions at the time of the alleged "first landing" of 1950 have now been checked and confirmed by the French police, whose investigators found the tiny farmhouse mentioned as the target of a burglary raid performed by the alleged "invaders." In the late sixties, UMMO had casually claimed that several objects, among them an electrical meter, had been "taken for study" in 1950. The police searched their old archives for months and found a complaint filed by the farmer for the disappearance of his electrical meter. However, they did not find the cave where other artifacts are supposedly hidden.

In August, 1974, I was driving a Renault on a narrow, forlorn little road up the precipitous valley of a mountain creek in the Alps. With me were Aimé Michel and Fernand Lagarde, two of the best-informed researchers of paranormal phenomena in Europe. We went as far as the road would lead us, to a tiny village where Michel engaged a local farmer in patois. We were looking for some indications that might confirm or disprove the UMMO story. The people in the village assured us there was no cave in the vicinity, and we went on to another village. After two days of inquiries in a small section of the mountains around La Javie we had located the area of the main events and compared notes with a friend who had conducted a similar search both on land and by air. (The

French Air Force too had taken pictures of the area and suspicious markings had been carefully investigated by search parties.)

Driving back along the precipice that day I was thinking of another celebrated case that had never been solved, another case of a UFO with an insignia. At Socorro, New Mexico, in 1964, officer Lonnie Zamora had seen an egg-shaped object in the desert, with two rather small men near it. On the side of this craft he had seen a peculiar red sign, a sort of vertical arrow with a horizontal bar underneath. No explanation for this sign was ever found. Then one afternoon I had brought up the subject in a conversation about folklore and mythology while visiting a friend at Stanford. He had been intrigued by my description of the Socorro symbol. It reminded him of something, he said. And after much searching among his numerous books he showed me a copy of a medieval Arabic text which included a list of symbols for the major planets: here, unmistakably, was the insignia Zamora had seen—the Arabic sign for Venus!

This is another reminder that one cannot understand the UFO phenomenon without taking into consideration all of its possible symbolic ramifications, no matter how seemingly remote from our technological reality. But the story of UMMO teaches us much more, as we slowly unravel the relationship between the reality of our beliefs and what we like to call the "objective" reality of our physics. The fact is that the beliefs of humanity can be manipulated both by physical and symbolic means. Certainly this is one of the objectives of UMMO, whether it is a prankish game, a psycho-sociological test or a sinister plot. But UMMO is only a small part of the total phenomenon, and the time has clearly come to assess the full impact of our strange, bewildering confrontation with it.

CHAPTER FIVE

The Confrontation

As the Sun shines down from Heaven
In a camera waiting waiting
As it heats my soul is shaking
Camera waiting waiting . . .
Golden chariots filling up the sky
Take us children to a golden high—

> Sunlight saves
> Moonlight saves
> High-light saves
> *It's made a witness of me!*

Take the lights right out of nothing
Let me tell you 'bout the way 'twill be
It burns brightest when ev'rybody's watching,
Oh—how wonderful:
We are saved!
Oh—How *wonderful!*
> —From *Sunlight Saves,*
> a song by John Musall, 1974.

Almost as if by accident, we seem to have come across something very important. We have encountered a multifaceted phenomenon and we are trying very hard to ignore it, because it does not fit into any neat category and refuses to be dragged under a microscope to be examined. Instead, it appears to seek confrontation with us *on its own terms*. What are these terms? What kind of human experience does a close encounter with a UFO constitute? And how can we ever obtain reports of the kind and quality that would be necessary to define the nature of the phenomenon?

Seven Categories of Strangeness

A farmer sees a light in the sky. A housewife is frightened by a disk-shaped object that dives toward her car on a lonely road. A man walking through the hills finds himself enveloped in a dense mist and wakes up in a daze at a spot many miles away, having no recollection of what he has done to get there. A young girl reports a blue flame that flickers in a nearby wood. A child of five tells the teacher that someday he will go to the stars with the little men in the red machine and, under questioning, reveals that last summer he played with a group of diminutive creatures who came out of a landed disk when he was alone on his grandmother's farm.

Such are the reports that are collected by the people who study the UFO problem: they vary greatly in the strangeness of the event, and it would be wrong to assume that all investigators receive approximately the same kind of information. There are significant differences between each one. Furthermore, each collection reflects a different investigator's method and bias. Official investigators, such as U.S. Air Force personnel or the police, tend to get all the reports of strange lights and aircraft-like objects. Amateur organizations and private researchers receive more landing and occupant reports than do the police.

This fact gave me a clue to what I regard as a fundamental problem in this type of research: *when scientists and the military discuss UFOs, they are not talking about the same part of the phenomenon the public perceives.* The antagonism with which UFO amateurs view the official researchers can to a large extent be explained by the fact that they literally "see" a different set of reports. If dif-

ferent investigators are so biased that most of them perceive only a fraction of the experiences they are attempting to study, then a scientific investigator will be faced
with serious problems simply in attempting to define the
boundaries of his research.

I will present here a framework for the reporting phenomenon that will clarify and reconcile these differences.
Then we will be able to see how the sighting reports re-
late to the framework.

A basic characteristic of the confrontation with a UFO is
the strangeness of the occurrence. Dr. Allen Hynek, in his
book *The UFO Experience* proposed a study of the
strangeness in connection with the reliability of a report.
Is it necessarily true, he asked, that the strangest reports
(such as the landing cases with occupants) always come
from the least reliable sources? He found that such was
NOT the case, and that many reports existed in his files
with *both* high reliability and high strangeness.

Let us take this idea one step further and discuss the
probability that a given witness will report seeing a UFO.
Assuming ten people have seen a strange object in the sky,
how many of these reports will I be able to obtain? This
depends, of course, on how willing each of the witnesses
will be to tell anyone about his experience, and also it will
depend on the person to whom he relates it. On this basis
I have defined seven categories of strangeness and I have
constructed for each category an appropriate scenario, as
follows:

Strangeness Category 1: You see a flickering light as you
come out of the garage. It reminds you of a firefly, but you
have never observed fireflies under quite similar conditions. *Result:* You are unlikely to call the police or the Air
Force to report this! If you do tell someone about the
sighting, it will probably be *a friend* or associate: "I didn't
know there were fireflies at this time of year."

Strangeness Category 2: As you come out of the garage

you see a flaming object that plunges behind the hill. Perhaps you have read somewhere that meteors and fireballs often appeared to be quite close when in fact they were hundreds of miles away. However, you call *the police* to report it because the summer has been very dry and you are afraid the phenomenon, whatever it is, may cause something to catch fire.

Strangeness Category 3: You put your car away and come out of the garage in time to see a luminous object giving off a blue glow that plunges behind the hill. It looks like a large, circular aircraft and seems to have some windows but no tail or wings. Could it be that the Russians are up to something? You call the nearest *Air Force* base to report it, out of a feeling of civic duty.

Strangeness Category 4: You park the old Chevy by the side of the barn and as you walk toward the house you suddenly see a large disk with lighted portholes that comes down with a gentle rocking motion and touches the ground near the pen where the pigs are kept. It makes a humming sound that turns into a high pitch whistle and it takes off again. You think of calling the police, but it occurs to you that the neighbors will be intrigued and the story will be all over the town the next day. You realize that the Air Force might be interested, but you think better of it when your wife tells you she read an article in a magazine explaining how the Air Force paid some big university to study those things and it came out negative. On the other hand, Joe down the street has lots of books on the subject and gets a little journal from a private UFO *group in Indiana.* Perhaps he would pass along the information to them. This way you could at least tell *someone* about it without being ridiculed.

Strangeness Category 5: As you lock the garage to make sure no vandals will scratch the paint on the new Corvette you are suddenly confronted with a dwarf wearing a silvery diving suit. It has no visible arms but its oversized eyes glow with a strange orange light. It turns around and walks stiffly away into the bushes. A moment later a round object takes off from behind the hedge. At first you are too shocked to move, but you come to your senses and go into the house. You tell *your wife* you don't feel like going on that camping trip next weekend. She wants to know why and you reluctantly tell her about what you've just seen, after she promises not to tell her mother.

Strangeness Category 6: You are lying in bed, wondering whether there is enough gas left in the car to drive to church and back tomorrow, when suddenly a light appears in the backyard. At the same time the baby starts crying in the next room. You get up in your pajamas to check the screen door and a large blue object comes into view, hovering six feet away. A beam of light appears underneath. It sweeps along the ground with a small white spot and comes toward you. When it hits your face thousands of thoughts come into your mind. You become "locked" within the strange light. A torrent of ideas seems to be transferred into your consciousness at a high rate. It suddenly stops and the blue object vanishes on the spot. You lean against the door wondering whether it was of God or the devil. Your mind is filled with burning questions. Could life exist on other planets? What if what we call God was only one of millions of higher beings who exist throughout the cosmos? You develop a throbbing headache. You take a sleeping pill and go back to bed without awakening your wife. The baby seems to have gone to sleep.

Strangeness Category 7: You are driving a truck at fifty miles an hour around a bend in the road when you become aware of a large, dark object that blocks the whole highway. There seems to be no possibility to avoid a collision but an invisible force appears to take hold of the fifteen-ton rig and bring it to a stop within a few feet of the object. A ring of smoke extends from the base of the dome-shaped craft and you start choking as it reaches the truck. The next thing you remember is that you are driving around another bend in the road fifty miles to the south. You look at your watch and it is an hour later than you thought it was.

These seven categories comprise the spectrum of encounters we have to deal with, and each one corresponds to a different probability of report and a different way of reporting. The following table summarizes the theory:

TABLE 1

Strangeness Category	Example	Estimated Probability of Report	Generally Reports to Whom?
1	"firefly"	1 in 10	anyone
2	burning mass	3 in 10	police
3	unknown craft	4 in 10	military
4	landing	2 in 10	local "expert"
5	occupant	1 in 10	close family
6	personal "illumination"	almost nil	no one
7	reality gap	almost nil	unconscious mind does not report it to conscious mind

Many examples of cases in the different categories could be given; the sightings of strangeness 4, 5, and 6 are especially interesting, but the witness of these sightings will report it only to a person he trusts. Dr. Hynek has shown me letters he has received from people saying "I am reporting this to you, but please do not report it to the Air Force!" Thus the witnesses were making a distinction between his image as an individual scientist and his role as a consultant to the military.

An example of a sighting in category 5 which has received a great deal of publicity is the 1964 Socorro case, in which a highway patrolman saw a white object and two rather small occupants. Although he did report it, he first asked to be left alone with a priest! The Betty and Barney Hill "abduction" case of 1961 is a fascinating one in light of this classification because one part of the incident (the observation of a disk with windows) is clearly of category 3 and this is indeed what they reported to the Air Force. They did not say anything about the creatures (category 5) or the time loss (category 7), which only came to light after they discussed the case with someone they trusted, a local UFO amateur. Finally, the whole story of their "abduction" only came out under hypnosis.

The Hilltop Curve

I call this the Hilltop Theory because when the data are set up as a graph the curve is somewhat shaped like a mountain (see Figure 1).

The interest of the Invisible College has moved from the officially reported cases (categories 2 and 3) to the harder to find sightings of strangeness 4 and 5. My own interest lies in the psychic cases of categories 6, 7, and cases that may even go beyond the chart entirely because we cannot yet think of a classification for them. I approach these cases with the cooperation of readers who have reacted to several articles I deliberately published in non-scientific journals; these articles addressed the unidentified cases that had been neatly swept under the rationalist rug.

The Hilltop Theory could be summed up in the statement that the type of data collected by an investigator is a function of his image (the beliefs about him) among his audience. It implies that scientists can only obtain a certain type of data (a biased sample). Similarly, the military and the amateur groups each perceive a different angle of the entire phenomenon. One can only learn more by changing one's own projected attitude, and that is what I have done.

The results of this experiment have been mixed, often

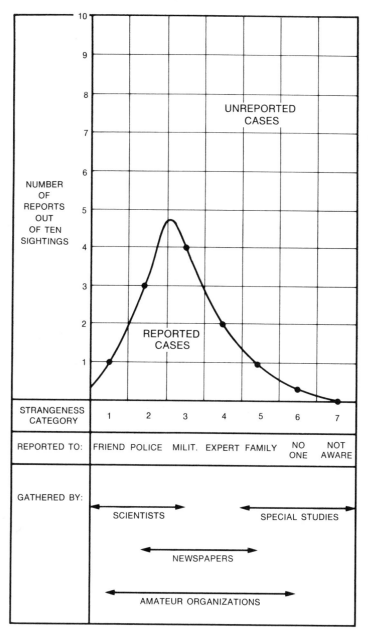

FIGURE 1

disappointing. I have been approached by many witnesses, some of whom were lying or crazy. I have been invited to join occult organizations. I have met individuals whose behavior fits none of the ordinary classifications. I have been in a position to verify observations that others like Jerome Clark and Donald Hanlon, Gordon Creighton and John Keel had made before me; although I do not buy all their conclusions I have convinced myself of the validity of their reports. The most interesting result of this experiment has been the establishment of contacts with individual scientists doing pioneering work in these border areas. *Nature,* the respected British magazine, has commented about these researchers in an editorial:

> It would have amazed the Victorian steadfasts of science how confused some of our attitudes towards science still are. Instead of the logical world they hoped for and tried to work in there is a discernible tendency for the public and even some practitioners of science to turn their backs on science and become preoccupied with the bizarre and the magical.[1]

The statement is an interesting one, because one might wonder how the Victorian steadfasts of science would have reacted when confronted with such *bizarre* concepts as infrared satellites, and *magical* devices like electronic computers (both technological developments against which some conservative scientists have fought long and hard because they thought they were mere engineering toys, and a waste of money). *I think there is a general shifting of man's belief patterns, his entire relationship to the concept of the invisible. It is happening outside of any established structure, and science is not immune to it.*

Two Letters

The scientists who compose the Invisible College are not easily intimidated by conservative attitudes. Genuine

1. "Science Beyond the Fringe," *Nature* 248 (April 12, 1974), p. 541.

science, they believe, is made by moving into unknown domains (even when they are guarded by those three fierce paper dragons, Bizarre, Magic, and Ridicule) armed with the belief that even the wierdest occurrence can eventually be reduced to a cause the human mind can understand. I have been especially interested in two letters containing criticisms of some statements I had published about encounters with UFOs; the first one came from Jerome Clark, a writer on psychic phenomena:

> Let me comment on your hypothesis that "contact between human percipients and the UFO Phenomenon occurs under conditions controlled by the latter." My view is just the opposite: namely, that the percipient controls the conditions. A striking illustration to what I mean comes from the dream of a young woman acquaintance who, knowing nothing of my views of the UFO phenomenon, told me that she had seen a little man step out of the craft. He was weeping plaintively—addressing the dreamer, he pleaded with her to "let him go." He said she had created him and he could not exist without her. Because she had given him form and personality, he was completely her slave. He was weeping for the freedom he would never have.

Another letter came from a medical doctor in Pennsylvania, a psychiatrist who is shifting his research efforts to psychic phenomena:

> I was startled by the seeming nonsense statements uttered on the part of some of the beings in the UFOs. Rather than look for the meaning of the absurd statements, I think you might seek another purpose for them, namely, that this is employed both as a hypnotic technique (i.e., the technique of confusion) and it is also employed for sending telepathic messages, and in some types of psychic healing.
>
> When the person is distracted by the absurd or contradictory, and their mind is searching for meaning, they are extremely open to thought transference, to receiving psychic healing, etc. Whatever they receive by way of

thought transference, of course becomes *their thought*, and they have no resistance to it. . . .

It would be interesting to see if a gifted psychic could determine what thoughts had been transmitted to them at the time of the nonsense statements, or if this could be determined through deep hypnosis.

These two letters have implications for the Hilltop Theory because they would affect our interpretation of the strangeness and the probability to report. If some encounters are in fact triggered by the witness himself (a hypothesis I do not at the moment accept because one cannot, as the first letter above does, generalize from a dream to the UFO descriptions under waking conditions) then we may be dealing with a combination of complex phenomena involving a psychic relationship between witnesses and the perceived objects, rather than a single UFO phenomenon coming from outside.

The second letter contains the provocative argument that absurdity is designed into UFO occurrences in order to permit thought transference while the mind is open to external influences. This would account for the low report probability in strangeness categories 6 and 7.

In Chapter One, I recounted the story of a witness who was asked the time by a UFO occupant. "It is 2:30," the witness replied.

"You lie; it is four o'clock."

I am indebted to Gerald Askevold for bringing to my attention an interesting book [2] which quotes a fascinating story by Dr. Milton Erickson concerning what the authors call "The Gentle Art of Reframing":

"One windy day . . . a man came rushing around the corner of a building and bumped hard against me as I stood bracing myself against the wind. Before he could recover his poise to speak to me, I glanced elaborately at my watch and courteously, as if he had inquired the time

2. P. Watzlawick, J. Weakland, and R. Rish, *Change: Principles of Problem Formation and Problem Resolution* (New York: Norton, 1974).

of day, I stated, 'It's exactly ten minutes of two,' though it was actually closer to 4 P.M., and walked on. About half a block away, I turned and saw him still looking at me, undoubtedly still puzzled and bewildered by my remark."

After quoting this story, the authors of *Change* continue:

This is how Erickson described the incident that led him to the development of an unusual method of hypnotic induction which he later called the Confusion Technique. What had taken place?

The incident of bumping into each other had created a context in which the obvious conventional response would have been mutual apologies. Dr. Erickson's response suddenly and unexpectedly redefined that same context as a very different one, namely, one that would have been socially appropriate if the other man had asked him the time of day, but even that would have been bewildering because of the patent incorrectness of the information, in contrast to the courteous, solicitous manner in which it was given. The result was confusion, unalleviated by any further information that would have re-organized the pieces of the puzzle into an understandable new frame of reference. As Erickson points out, the need to get out of the confusion by finding this new frame makes the subject particularly ready and eager to hold on firmly to the next piece of concrete information that he is given. The confusion, setting the stage for reframing, thus becomes an important step in the process of effecting second-order change and of "showing the fly the way out of the fly-bottle."

Was the alleged "UFO pilot" trying to show the witness the way out of a similar maze? Is this Confusion Technique deliberately used to effect change on a major scale? This could also help us to understand the strong resemblance that anyone who has examined the beliefs of esoteric groups could not fail to note between certain UFO encounters and the initiation rituals of secret societies. This "opening of the mind" to a new set of symbols that is reported by many witnesses is precisely what the various occult traditions are also trying to achieve.

The Case of José Antonio

A case in point is the story of José Antonio, an enlisted Brazilian soldier (No. 33930) in the military police of Minas Gerais and orderly to Major Celio Ferreira, who commanded at that time a Guard's Battalion. An investigation conducted by Mr. Brant Aleixo and published in the *Flying Saucer Review* (Nov./Dec., 1973) disclosed that one Sunday afternoon in May, 1969, José Antonio was fishing on a lagoon north of Belo Horizonte when he suddenly became aware of figures moving behind him. He saw a "burst of light" hit his legs and felt a numbness that caused him to drop his fishing rod and fall to his knees. He was seized by two masked individuals about four feet tall, wearing dull aluminum suits, who took him to a machine that looked like an upright cylinder. Inside this craft the beings gave him a helmet similar to their own, tied him up, and took off:

> The higher the machine seemed to rise, the more difficult did breathing seem for the soldier, and at one stage, in addition to his state of low morale, he felt as though his whole body was physically tired out, almost paralyzed. He felt more and more uncomfortable in this position, owing to the hardness and the shape of the seat, the numbness in his legs, and the weight of the helmet, the corners of which were bruising his shoulders and neck.

After a period of travel which seemed "interminable," the machine landed with a jarring sensation and the little men unfastened José Antonio. They put a bandage over the eyeholes in his helmet and carried him with his knees dragging on the ground. He heard footsteps and the sound of many people talking. Finally he was placed on a backless seat and the bandage was removed.

José Antonio found himself in a large quandrangular
room, thirty by forty feet, about fifteen feet away from a
robust dwarf who stared at him "with apparent satisfaction." He was extremely hairy:

> His long tresses, reddish and wavy, fell down behind
> past his shoulders to his waist; his beard was long and
> thick and came down to his stomach. He had wide-set
> eyebrows, two fingers thick, running right across the
> whole forehead. His skin was light-colored, very pale.
> His eyes were round, larger than is the norm with us,
> and of a green shade like the color of green leaves
> beginning to wither.

Other beings of similar appearance began arriving until
about fifteen dwarfs were in the room. The soldier assumed there was a door in the back beyond his field of
vision. The three walls he could see had no window and
no door.

To his left was a low shelf with the corpses of four men,
one of them a Negro. He thought they had been killed by
the homunculi. The whole room seemed to be made of
stone, and at one point he was given something to drink
out of a cubical stone glass, and the cavity containing a
dark green liquid was *in the shape of an inverted pyramid.*

The lighting in the room was uniform and intensely
bright, coming from no identifiable source. On the left
wall were paintings of animals: a jaguar, a monkey, a
giraffe, an elephant; also vehicles, houses, etc. In the far
right angle of the room was something that looked like an
upside-down racing car.

He watched while the homunculi examined all his fishing equipment and carefully took *one of every item in duplicate:* they kept one specimen of each type of fishing
hook and a single banknote from a total of 35,000 old cru-
zeiros.

The leader of the dwarfs began a strange conversation
with the soldier. It was entirely conducted through ges-

tures and drawings and revolved around the concept of weapons. (José Antonio thinks that they must have perceived that he was in the military and illustrated this by their actions.) At one time a little man shot a beam of light against the stone wall. The communication seemed to be a request that José Antonio help the little beings in their relations with earth. Was he to be their guide among men? This is what José Antonio understood. He gestured his refusal and began praying, fingering the rosary he always carried with him:

> The leader stepped towards him and, displaying irritation for the first time, seized the crucifix and snatched it from him. One of the beads rolled onto the floor and was picked up by one of the little men, who showed it to the others. The crucifix was passed around in the same way, arousing the curiosity of all of them.

While this discussion took place among the homunculi José Antonio had a vision of a Christ-like entity, "his eyes clear and serene," barefoot and wearing a dark robe. The figure made some revelations to José Antonio, who now refuses to disclose them. The apparition vanished, the irritated dwarfs blindfolded him again, and he was transported back. As the machine landed, he felt that he was being dragged and he lost consciousness. He woke up alone, near the town of Vitoria in the state of Espirito Santo, two hundred miles away from the spot where he had been fishing. He had been away for four and a half days.

Out of the Body

There is a curious parallel to this case in the experiences of Robert Monroe, an American businessman who systematically investigates out-of-the-body travel (see Chapter Six). On a particular occasion he had the feeling of being outside his body, fighting with two small beings:

Desperate for a solution, I thought about fire and this seemed to help a little. However, I got the impression that they were both amused, as if there was nothing I could do to harm them. By this time, I was sobbing for help.

Then I saw someone else coming up out of the corner of my eye. I first thought it was another one, but this was very definitely a man. He simply stopped a short distance away and watched what was taking place with a very serious expression on his face. . . . He wore a dark robe down to his ankles. I could not see his feet.

As in the case of José Antonio, the apparition of the taller man was the signal for the end of the ordeal.

Initiation rituals are characterized by the following phases or general scenes, often combined or developed into complex themes:

1. The candidate is confronted by members of the group wearing special costumes.

2. He is blindfolded.

3. He is led by the arm through a rough and difficult route.

4. He is taken into a specially designed chamber that has no windows and is placed in such a way that he can only see part of it.

5. He is placed in the presence of a "Master."

6. He is given a test and made to answer questions.

7. He is shown a variety of symbols designed to remind him of death.

8. The situation suggests that he may not survive the ordeal.

9. He is given ritual food.

10. He is blindfolded again and led outside.

All of these elements are present in the case of José Antonio. To this we must add the fact that everything in the room appeared to be made out of stone. The drinking cube with the inverted pyramid cavity is an exquisite last touch.

In interpreting such a case we must remember that it

took place in South America, a place where occultism thrives and where religion often takes the form of intense mystical passion.

The Case of Paulo Gaetano

Another remarkable case from South America will close this chapter, raising additional possibilities for the nature of confrontation.

On November 17, 1971, at 9:30 P.M. a Brazilian man named Paulo Gaetano was driving back from the town of Natividade de Carangola on a business trip. With him in the car was another man, Mr. Elvio B. As they passed the town of Bananeiras, Paulo felt the car was not pulling normally, and mentioned it to his companion, who reacted by saying only that he was tired and wanted to sleep. The engine stalled and Paulo had to stop the car on the side of the road. He then saw an object about twelve feet away. A red beam of light was projected at the car and "caused the door to open." Several small beings appeared, took Paulo into the craft, and made him lie down on a small table. Fastening his arms, they lowered from the ceiling an apparatus that resembled an X-ray machine. He felt a cut near his elbow and they collected his blood. (Investigators from the SBEVD research group in Brazil saw and photographed the wound three days later.) Then he was shown two panels, one of them a plan of the town of Itaperuna, the other a picture of an atomic explosion. Paulo felt heavy. He remembers being helped by Elvio, but does not recall how they got back home.

The interesting point is that the witness was not alone. Did Elvio also see the flying saucer? No. He only saw a *bus*:

> Near Bananeires, Paulo had begun to show signs of nervousness, Elvio reported. He told him that there was a flying saucer accompanying them, when in fact what was

following them was a *bus* which was keeping at a rea-
sonable distance behind the car.

Elvio added that the car had slowed down and stopped,
and that he had come to the assistance of Paulo after he
had fallen to the ground, behind the car, with the door on
the driver's side remaining open. Elvio managed to get
Paulo on his feet and started with him by bus toward Itaperuna, where Paulo was examined by the first-aid station.
The police sent a patrol to the site and found Paulo's car
on the highway. Elvio was unable to explain what had
happened to Paulo and why the door was open. He did not
remember when Paulo had gotten out. And he could not
explain why they had taken the bus. The police found no
trace on the car that could explain the *wound* on Paulo's
arm.

It is becoming technically feasible for sounds and
images to be projected into people's minds at a distance. Is
this part of the technology that creates the UFO phenomenon? Could the required equipment be carried on board
an ordinary bus? Here again we must ask the question first
posed at the occasion of the UMMO investigation: Are we
dealing with a terrestrial technology that systematically
confuses the witnesses? If so, it must be possible to demonstrate it. If certain areas of the human brain can be remotely stimulated, then it is not impossible to think of
broadcasts literally saturating large territories with a flood
of symbols. Such a device could be a major tool of social
change. If disguised under a preposterous or "absurd" appearance, its effects would be undetected for a long time. I
believe this could be a key to the confrontation with
UFOs.

CHAPTER SIX

The Winged Disk

> In the last analysis magic, religion and science are
> nothing but theories of thought; and as science has sup-
> planted its predecessors, so it may hereafter be itself
> superceded by some more perfect hypothesis, perhaps
> by some totally different way of looking at the pheno-
> mena—of registering the shadows on the screen—of
> which we in this generation can form no idea.
>
> —Sir James Frazer, O.M.,
> *The Golden Bough*

The problem before us now is this: If the reality behind
the UFO phenomenon is both physical *and psychic* in nature, and if it manipulates space and time in ways our scientific concepts are inadequate to describe, is there any
reason for its effects to be limited to our culture or to our
generation? We have already established that no country
has had the special privilege of these manifestations, and
we have speculated about sightings made before World
War II. Yet we must carry the argument further: If the
UFO phenomenon is not tied to social conditions specific
to our time, or to technological achievements like atom
bombs and rockets, then it may represent a universal fact.
It may have been with us, in one form or another, as long
as the human race has existed on this planet.

In a previous book (*Passport to Magonia*) I offered the
view that much of human folklore could be usefully re-ex-
amined from this angle. In fact, in the six years that have

elapsed since the publication of that book, evidence of a similar body of beliefs in practically all human cultures has been mounting. Not only are beings similar to the modern-day "occupants" described in old legends from all parts of the world, but vehicles endowed with the same properties as the UFOs occupy a prominent part in some stories (such as the "Wheels" of Ezekiel, the flying chariots of the legends of India, the round baskets from heaven in American Indian folklore, the "flying shields" of the Romans, the "cloudships from Magonia" of medieval French chronicles, the "illuminated flying houses" of the Celtic fairy-folks, etc.).

In this chapter I will examine some of the lessons that can be drawn from the existence of entities similar to what we call UFOs, and I will introduce some new indications that belief in the possibility of "contact" with these entities may have represented a religious turning point. Finally, I will discuss the role that the "beam of light" symbol plays in connection with these entities, and I will trace these symbols from ancient to modern times.

Something happened in classical times that is very inadequately explained by historical theories. The suggestion that the same thing might be happening again should make us extremely interested in bringing every possible light to bear on this problem. What I am referring to is the collapse of ancient civilizations.[1] Beginning in the second century B.C. and continuing until the fall of the Roman Empire the intellectual elites of the Mediterranean world, raised in a spirit of scientific rationalism, were confronted and eventually defeated by an irrational element similar to that contained in modern apparitions of unexplained phenomena, an element that is dramatized in their summary rejection by our own science.

Commenting upon this parallel, Aimé Michel suggests

1. See in particular the data contained in Nilsson, *Greek Piety* (New York: Norton, 1969) and Dodd, *The Greeks and the Irrational* (Berkeley: U. of California Press, 1959).

that we picture the following scene: Take one of the Alex-
andrine thinkers, a man like Ptolemaeus, thoroughly
schooled in the rational methods of Archimedes, Euclid,
and Aristotle. And imagine him reading the Apocalypse (or
any of the numerous versions that were then circulating).
How would he react to such an experience? He would
merely shrug, says Aimé Michel: "It would never occur to
him to place the slightest credence in such a compendium
of what he must regard as insanities. Such a scene must
have taken place thousands of times at the end of classical
antiquity. And we know that every time there was the
same rejection, the same shrugging, because we have no
record of *any* critical examination of the doctrines, ideas,
and claims of the counterculture that expressed itself
through the Apocalypse. This counterculture was too *absurd* to retain the attention of a reader of Plato. A short
time—a very short time—elapsed, the counterculture
triumphed, and Plato was forgotten for a thousand years. Is
this what is happening again?"

The question posed by Aimé Michel is vast and complex. We must seek the elements of an answer in those
characteristics of the phenomenon that can be reliably
traced from ancient to modern times. In spite of much popular interest in the mysterious monuments of South
America that Eric Von Daniken has tried to link with
space visitors, it is in the Middle East that we find the
most relevant indications of a cultural change similar to
the one we are undergoing.

Phoenician Amulets

History books tell us that the Phoenician civilization was
established at a time much anterior to the Hebrew migra-
tions, when several Semitic tribes founded a series of
cities on the Mediterranean littoral: the main ones were
known as Tyre, Sidon, Tripoli, Byblos, and each was governed by an oligarchy or by a king. At the height of its development, Phoenicia itself extended through that part of

Syria that goes from Nahr-al-Kabir (Eleutherus) on the north to Mount Carmel on the south.

The language of the Phoenicians was close to Hebrew (it descended from the old Canaanite language) and their alphabet, possibly the oldest form of Semitic writing, is generally regarded as the predecessor of the Greek and Latin alphabets and, indirectly, of all Western alphabets. It may itself have derived from either Babylonian characters or from Egyptian hieroglyphs.

Sir E. A. Wallis Budge, one of this century's most distinguished scholars on Egypt and Mesopotamia, states that the Phoenicians were not a literary people. Unlike most Semitic peoples, the Phoenicians loved the sea. They used their abundant forests to supply the timber for their ships. Their work was exceptionally refined and their products were sold by their merchants throughout the ancient world, in Europe, Asia, Africa, and India. They had learned from Babylon the art of dyeing, from Egypt the craft of glassblowing, and they used accurate systems of weights. Little is known of their religious beliefs, although it is often pointed out, on linguistic grounds, that the names of their gods showed direct Babylonian, Egyptian, and Greek influnces.

Of their ritual practices we are told that they sacrificed their first-born children in times of trouble; that they similarly killed their prisoners of war on the altars of their gods; and that their women surrendered their virginity in the sanctuaries of Astarte. For their personal magical protection the Phoenicians appear to have adopted the type of amulets used in Babylonia and Assyria, and a collection of cylinder-seals has been preserved in the British Museum (Department of Egyptian and Assyrian Antiquities). Some of these artifacts, which are shown in the following figures, A through E, may date from a few centuries B.C., probably from about 400 to 300 B.C. *All five of these cylinder seals depict the Winged Disk, often with appendages. Figures which are referred to in the literature as "divine beings" are seen emerging from these disks in four cases. And in every one of them human figures in ceremonial dress appear to be involved in rituals that contain Assyrian features.*

Figure A

This cylinder seal shows a hero holding in each hand the foreleg of a winged beast. One of these two beasts (the one on the right) has horns on its head, and a tail. Above the human being is the winged disk, from which a god is emerging. ("Ahuramazda or some Assyrian god," writes Sir Wallis Budge.)

Figure B

The interpretation of this amulet, as given in Sir Wallis Budge's book *Amulets and Superstitions*,[2] involves scorpion-men and sexual symbols. It is apparent that two strange creatures, obviously males, are supporting a winged disk above a sacred tree. To the right is a worshipper, while another person is bringing some sort of animal as a sacrifice. Here, again, two divine figures are to be seen, emerging from the disk. The inscription reads: "Belonging to PLTHAN."

2. Published in the U.S. as *Amulets and Talismans* (New York: Collier, 1970).

Figure C

Two large winged figures—classically interpreted as "priests wearing winged garments"—frame a large disk with extended legs; directly beneath the disk is a symbol of lightning or thunderbolt, before which a man appears to be standing in adoration. There is something on top of the disk, which is interpreted by authorities as "a lion's head."

The inscription reads: "YRPAL, the son of HR'DD."

Figure D

A sphinx and a goat stand on either side of a sacred tree above which is a winged disk. Two men are performing a ritual in connection with the scene.

Figure E

Again, two of the strange dwarfish figures which authorities call scorpion-men (despite their quite obvious breasts on this particular seal) are supporting a "winged disk from which project the heads of three divine beings." Two men are in adoration before the disk, beneath which a sort of vaulted door can be seen. To the left is a very strange figure interpreted as "a god holding a gazelle or goat under each arm."

All five seals are about one inch high.

The interpretation of this collection of artifacts raises several questions, because the classical statement that the flying disk is simply a primitive representation of the sun or the soul leaves much to be desired. In the first place, is it common for the winged disk (a frequent symbol in antiquity) to show several beings emerging from its upper part? In what context are such representations encountered? If

the disk is interpreted as some mythological symbol connected with the cosmos (as is indicated by the abundance of astronomical symbols in the seals: stars, crescent moons), should we think of the appendages of the disk in terms other than biological? In other words, should we speculate that the representation of a disk with extended claws may in fact seek to preserve the memory of a vision, or observation, of a flying craft capable of landing, of the type so frequently described in more recent history?

Tempting as it is, this speculation does not answer all our questions either, but it provides a stimulating avenue of research into ancient symbolism. It is certainly fascinating to read that the best accepted interpretation for the zigzag symbol in Figure C is lightning or a thunderbolt. Why should a thunderbolt be associated with a winged disk, and why should three people in elaborate magical garments stand in adoration before it? The scene suggests plan and purpose rather than a chance occurrence of some purely natural phenomenon.

Equally fascinating to the student of close-encounter UFO cases are the scenes in which animals are carried to the hovering disk, as in Figures B and E: in the latter case, a god is seen holding some horned animal under each arm—a scene certainly reminiscent of Hamilton's cow [3] and many a claim of animal kidnapping by UFO occupants. Three of the cylinder seals (B, D, E) show approximately the same thing: a disk above some elaborate ground structure: a human in adoration: someone bringing a horned animal toward the center of the scene.

The beings themselves fall into the following categories:

1. Human beings that Assyriologists call "worshippers," "priests," "kings," etc. Sometimes they are wearing winged garments.

2. The gods. They are shown either emerging from the disk, and wearing in some cases elaborate headdresses, or walking outside the disk, as in Figure E, where the entity at the left seems to be wearing its hair in three long tresses on either side of the head.

3. The scorpion-men, who have phallic attributes in Figure B but in Figure E would more properly be called scorpion-women; they are only seen supporting the disk. It would be interesting to find out where the word scorpion comes from in connection with these figures. The scorpion-men are consistently about two-thirds of the size of men, who in turn are smaller than the gods. (Professor Price-Williams, of UCLA, points out that in the Gilgamesh epic the scorpion creatures were the guardians of the mountain of the sun. The scorpion-man in the Babylonian Enuma Elish was a monster created by chaos at the beginning of the world. He adds: "These creatures would thus be tellurian beings, 'chthonic' as Jung would have said.")

4. Various monsters, such as the horned creature in Figure A, the sphinx in Figure D, etc.

Some important questions were left unanswered by an

---

3. In April, 1897, a farmer named Hamilton, together with several other people, saw the "hideous" occupants of an "airship" lift one of his cows aboard their craft. The butchered remains of the animal were later dropped in a field. [See *Anatomy of a Phenomenon* by Jacques Vallee (Chicago: Regnery, 1965), p. 16.]

interpretation of the scenes shown on the cylinder seals as actual flying craft. If we assume that the Phoenicians were thus transmitting recent or ancient knowledge of the details of UFO landings, why should such knowledge be preserved in seals rather than in other types of inscription? Of what importance would be such a reference as "YRPAL, the son of HR'DD," who was probably the owner of a glassblowing shop somewhere in Sidon, or perhaps the captain of a sailing ship from the harbor of Tyre?

On the other hand, why should the observation of a flying disk be represented in the context of an obviously magical ceremony that does not appear to have any traditional characteristic of Phoenician religion? We are told, for instance, that the Phoenicians held the same view as the Hebrews concerning the survival of the soul, that they buried their dead with great care, and that their sacrificial ceremonies involved the killing of human beings and sacred prostitution. Why then is it that, if the seals are associated with spiritual or religious values, they depict nothing of this, but do instead show winged disks which appear to come from a star, which contain strange beings who carry off earth animals, and which emit lightning bolts? And why are the human assistants wearing special vestments with wings on them?

One cannot build a complete theory of the similarity between ancient concepts and modern phenomena from a single set of symbols because they are subject to a variety of interpretations.[4] Nevertheless, such elements deserve to be patiently pursued, and the winged disk should be tracked down.

Representations of flying disks in religion do not stop with the Phoenicians. The symbol is a basic one in the early years of the Christian church, and it is consistently associated with the angels. Official Christian theology

4. I am well aware, in particular, that the flying disk has often been used to symbolize the winged soul. It is also associated with the serpent and with the caduceus (healing symbol).

does not have much to say about the angels, just as official Muslim theology remains discreet about the djinns. Some rare documents, however, give details concerning the nature of these beings. According to Japanese researcher Y. Matsumura, the religious *Sophia,* a written document commenting upon the dogma of the Greek Orthodox Church preserved in the Leningrad National Library, describes the process of communication between God and the angels:

> How does the Lord guide His Angel, if the Angel cannot see the face of His Lord? An Angel has a projection on the upper part of his eyes, where a sacred cloud rests. He has also a thing to receive sounds on his head. This thing makes noises as an Angel receives an order where to go from his Lord. Then he quickly looks at the mirror in his hand, and he gets in the mirror something on which an instruction from God is given.

I have not been able to verify directly the existence of this document and the accuracy of the translation, but it is consistent with a number of paintings, icons, and murals that depict contact between "God" and His messengers and contact between the messengers and men. Communication has for a long time taken place through pictorial representation rather than words, and it is not overly surprising to find few descriptions of such contact in written language.

I am inclined to a literal, rather than purely symbolic interpretation of the scenes depicted on the Phoenician amulets, and I am also tempted to accept as a working hypothesis that in other times remote contact occurred between human consciousness and another consciousness, variously described as demonic, angelic, or simply alien. This would explain much of the symbolic power retained in our own time by the concept of "signs in the sky." It would account for the fact that modern-day UFOs seem to present archaic as well as futuristic designs (as in the representation of the Arabic astrological sign for Venus on the object seen at Socorro), and it would also explain the fascination which people of all countries and races have always had for the strange entities from "above."

How constant these observations and visions have remained will be seen by comparing the Phoenician seal story with the following letter from a woman who saw a Scorpion-man in our own time.

The Case of the Oxford Scorpion-Man

A letter from a British woman:

> At the lecture by Jacques Vallee at the London A. A. [Architects' Association] on the 12th of December I was surprised by one of the slides of a Phoenician seal showing a winged sphere held up by two creatures which he described as "Scorpion men." Perhaps I have seen such a man myself, perhaps not, but I will tell you what I saw. . . .
>
> In the summer of 1968, I was driving home from London to a place near Stratford to visit some friends for the weekend. I had a companion in the car with me. Just outside Oxford, near Burford, we both saw a shining disk in the sky (it was around four in the afternoon and the sun was quite high). The disk was about the same size as the full moon in the evening. We slowed, and then stopped the car to watch it while it darted and dodged and swung about in the sky, almost as though showing off its abilities, we thought. Another car stopped to watch too. Eventually it sank down behind the trees, and we drove on.
>
> During the drive between Burford and Stratford I had some startling, and to me, novel insights into what I can only describe as the Nature of Reality. They were connected in some way to this shining disk, and have had a profound effect on me, causing what is commonly known as a personality change. I won't try to explain what those insights were since almost all the religions of the world have tried to do this and have failed. (In that afternoon I changed from an agnostic to a gnostic, if that means any-

thing at all.) However, these insights hit me like bolts from the blue, as though from outside, one after the other. I've never had a similar experience since.

That evening, after supper, we were in the sitting room which had open french-windows leading out onto the lawn. At one point I went over to the windows to get a breath of fresh air (it was very hot and close). The light from the room shone in an arc of about ten feet around the window. In that area I saw, as soon as I came to the window, a strange figure. My perception of it was heightened by the state of frozen panic it produced in me. It was for me without any doubt, a demon, or devil because of my Western oriented interpretation (I imagine) of the vision or creature or animal or man, or whatever it was I saw. Like the "Scorpion man," as well as Pan, it had dog or goat-like legs. It was covered in silky, downey fur, dark, and glinting in the light. It was unmistakably humanoid, and to my mind malevolent. It crouched, and stared, unblinkingly, at me with light, grape-green eyes that slanted upwards and had no pupils. The eyes shone and were by far the most frightening thing about it. It was, I think retrospectively, trying to communicate with me, but my panic interfered with any message I might have received. If it had stood to its full height it would have been about four to five feet tall. It had pointed ears and a long muzzle. It gave the impression of emaciation; its hands and fingers were as thin as sticks.

Eventually, convinced that I was hallucinating, I went and sat down for a while, until the panic had subsided. Then I went to see if it was still there. It was, except that it had moved further into the shadows on the edge of the arc of light. I made sure I kept away from that door for the rest of the evening, and left the next day. I told no one. That it may have been connected with the shining disk I only realized when I saw that slide.

The Beam of Light

A major feature in all religious traditions is that of the beam of light, emanating from a point in the sky or from a cloud of peculiar shape, and focused upon a human being.

This beam usually is a sign of "blessing" and conveys information from a divine source.

I am intrigued by this concept because it is a recurrent one in modern contact cases. We have seen this beam in action in the case of Dr. X and of Uri Geller. Another psychic experimenter, Mr. Robert Monroe, has described a similar phenomenon in his own investigations of out-of-the-body consciousness.[5] On the night of September 9, 1960, as he was lying on his bed, Mr. Monroe says:

> I suddenly felt bathed in and transfixed by a very powerful beam that seemed to come from the North, about 30° above the horizon. I was completely powerless, with no will of my own, and I felt as if I were in the presence of a very strong force, in personal contact with it.
>
> It had intelligence of a form beyond my comprehension, and it came directly (down the beam?) into my head, and seemed to be searching every memory in my mind. I was truly frightened because I was powerless to do anything about this intrusion.

On September 16, at night, again from the verbatim notes of Robert Monroe:

> The same impersonal probing, the same power, from the same angle. However, this time I received the firm impression that I was inextricably bound by loyalty to this intelligent force, always had been, and that I had a job to perform here on earth. . . .
>
> I got the impression of huge pipes, so ancient they were covered with undergrowth and rust. Something like oil was passing through them, but it was much higher in energy than oil, and vitally needed and valuable elsewhere (assumption: not on this material planet).

On September 30, the same pattern:

> They seemed to soar up into the sky, while I called after them, pleading. Then I was sure that their mentality and

5. In his excellent book, *Journeys Out of the Body* (New York: Doubleday, 1972).

intelligence were far beyond my understanding. It is an impersonal, cold intelligence, with none of the emotions of love or compassion which we respect so much, yet this may be the omnipotence we call God. Visits such as these in mankind's past could well have been the basis for all of our religious beliefs, and our knowledge today could provide no better answers than we could a thousand years past.

By this time, it was getting light, and I sat down and cried, great deep sobs and I have never cried before, because then I knew without any qualification or future hope of change that the God of my childhood, of the churches, of religion throughout the world was not as we worshipped him to be—that for the rest of my life, I would "suffer" the loss of this illusion.

The Case of the Tranquilizing Light

A case that took place in March, 1958, and was later reported in the pages of the *Flying Saucer Review* by French investigator Joel Mesnard provides an opportunity to verify again the strange properties of the lights associated with the UFO phenomenon in modern as in ancient times.

The witness here is a 28-year-old French Legionnaire who was on sentry duty at the Algerian camp of Bouahmama, in the desert south of Constantine. Shortly after 12:30 A.M. this man heard a whistling noise that seemed to be coming from the sky, and as he looked up he saw a very large object, about one thousand feet in diameter, coming down some one hundred fifty feet away from him. The most remarkable thing about this object, however, was not its enormous size but the intense conical beam of emerald-green light that came down from its underside (as in the case of Dr. X mentioned in Chapter One).

The recollections of the Legionnaire beyond this point are vague and, by his own admission, may not correspond to reality. Instead of either firing his gun to alert others or picking up the telephone to call his superiors, he re-

mained staring at the object for over three-quarters of an
hour. According to this man, as interviewed by Joel Mesnard: "The pale green and emerald colors were the most
beautiful, relaxing and fascinating colors he had ever
seen." [6]

The object departed in the most classical way: first the
whistling noise, then the rising to an altitude of about
three hundred feet, and finally the climb at "tremendous
speed" toward the northwest. As the object left and the
man returned to full awareness, the happy, ecstatic feeling
he had experienced was replaced by a feeling of sadness.
He picked up the telephone and reported what he had
seen to his superiors. They initially thought that the experience was a hallucination due to stress, but it is to the
great credit of the French military that a thorough investigation was pursued. Instead of sweeping the case under
the rug (and the French Legion in Algeria had more pressing problems at that time than investigating UFO landings!) the officers went to the site, examined it carefully,
found no physical evidence, resumed their questioning of
the witness, and, as he kept insisting on the veracity of the
event and they had no reason to doubt his truthfulness,
they sent him to Paris for a more detailed examination. In
Paris he was kept under observation for one week at the
Val-de-Grace Military Hospital. An electroencephalogram
revealed nothing unusual. The medical staff concluded
that he was in a state of good mental and physical health,
and did not suffer from the strain of war in any unusual
way.

Mr. Mesnard met the witness in May, 1970. He had returned to civilian life and impressed the investigator with
his practical, down-to-earth sense. He had been looking
for no publicity whatsoever and was even reluctant to
discuss his experience. When he did so, he answered
questions in a straight, matter-of-fact way. He has had no

6. Joel Mesnard, "Tranquilizing Visitation at Bouahmama," *Flying
Saucer Review* (May, 1973), p. 17.

illness of any kind since the day of the sighting, has had no new experience of an unusual type, and remains in the extremely peaceful state induced by the presence of the object. "It was like time running very slowly . . . it was like being in another world."

Is the mechanism of UFO apparitions, then, an invariant in all cultures? Are we faced here with something more than a projection of Jung's archetypal images, a psychic technology whose applications know few if any limitations in space and in time? I see no better hypothesis at this point of our knowledge of UFO phenomena. Certainly the space visitors hypothesis fails to explain adequately the ancient symbolism. We do not have a simple series of incidents that could be explained as an encounter with space travelers who might have spotted the earth and explored it casually on their way to another cosmic destination. Instead, we have a pattern of manifestations, opening the gates to a spiritual level, pointing a way to a different consciousness, and producing irrational, absurd events in their wake.

The Phoenician amulets, the close encounters with "occupants" in our time, the ancient beam from heaven, and the focused light from UFOs seem to imply a technology capable of both physical manifestation and psychic effects, a technology that strikes deep at the collective consciousness, confusing us, molding us—as perhaps it confused and molded human civilizations at the end of antiquity.

CHAPTER SEVEN

A Morphology of Miracles

And behold a new miracle.

There appeared a very great cloud over the bier like the great circle that useth to be seen about the splendour of the moon; and a host of angels was in the cloud sending forth a song of sweetness, and the earth resounded with the noise of that great melody.

Then the people came out of the city, about fifteen thousand, and marvelled and said:

What is the sound of such sweetness?

. . . But the angels that were in the clouds smote the people with blindness.

—The Apocryphal New Testament

What Happened at Fatima

The descriptions in the preceding chapter and the other phenomena we have discussed seem to point to an unsettling observation that forces us to deal simultaneously with two categories we always attempt to separate: the technical (or physical) and the spiritual (or divine). Many witnesses, in their statements after a close encounter with UFOs, claim that the experience of the phenomenon has a religious meaning to them. Perhaps it does. Perhaps we need, not only a scientific breakthrough here but a consciousness breakthrough as well, a global historical grasp of the beliefs—materialistic as well as idealistic—among which we have been groping for ten thousand years.

The famous apparitions at Fatima offer a historical example of the religious dimension of UFO encounters. The case is a celebrated one, yet I am prepared to wager that few American readers know the full story of what happened in 1917 near that small Portuguese town. I suspect that even fewer realize that the entire sequence of observations of an entity thought to be the Holy Virgin had begun two years previously with a fairly classical sequence of UFO sightings.

If we accept the interpretation given of Fatima by the Catholic Church, we are dealing with a phenomenon that cannot be explained either as a physical effect or as an illusion. In its decision of 1930, arrived at after thirteen years of painstaking investigations by many scholars, the Church states that:

> The solar phenomenon of the 13th of October 1917, described in the press of the time, was most marvelous and caused the greatest impression on those who had the happiness of witnessing it. . . .
>
> This phenomenon, which no astronomical observatory registered and which therefore was not natural, was witnessed by persons of all categories and of all social classes, believers and unbelievers, journalists of the principal Portuguese newspapers and even by persons some miles away. Facts which annul any explanation of collective illusion.

This "miracle," the reader will note, had been predicted several months before by three illiterate children after their vision of a woman "in a bright glow." She had not said that she was the Virgin Mary. She had simply stated that she was "from Heaven" and instructed them to return every month until October, when a public miracle would take place "so that everyone may believe."

The events at Fatima involve luminous spheres, lights with strange colors, a feeling of "heat waves," all physical characteristics commonly associated with UFOs. They even include the typical "falling-leaf" motion of the saucer zigzagging through the air. But they also encompass healing and prophecy and a loss of ordinary consciousness on the part of witnesses—what we have called the psychic component of UFO sightings. In one of the encounters a prophetic message was given to the children, and transmitted by them to the Church. A part of that message was not to be revealed until 1960, at which time Pope John XXIII opened the sealed envelope, but did not publish the secret. Some indirect information on the circumstances of this opening of the message, which I have obtained, sheds light on the reactions of high Church officials to the prophecy, if not on its actual contents. But let us now take the events in sequence.

The Pattern of Prophecy

The first apparition of the woman took place on May 13, 1917. Three children were watching their sheep when a bright flash surprised them, and they walked toward the large hollow pasture called Cova da Iria (literally: the Cave of St. Irene, *an old sacred spot*) to see what had happened. They found themselves caught in a glowing light that almost blinded them, and in the center of the light they perceived a little woman, who spoke to them, begging them to return every month to the same spot.

While the children had been alone on the first occasion, there were fifty people the second time, on June 13. They watched while the little shepherds knelt and became transfigured, as if transported into another world, at the time of the observation. The oldest child, Lucia, who was 10 at the time, addressed an unseen entity whose answers were not heard by others in the group. One spectator, however, reported perceiving a very faint voice or the buzzing of a bee (a typical sound associated with modern-day UFOs). At the end of the dialogue all witnesses heard an explosion and saw a small cloud rise from the vicinity of a tree—on which all the succeeding manifestations would center.

The following month, on July 13, the number of witnesses had risen to forty-five hundred! This third apparition was especially remarkable in several respects. It included detailed descriptions by some of the spectators of physical phenomena that are specific enough to be compared to UFO data:

> . . . a buzzing or humming sound, a decrease in the Sun's glow and heat, a small whitish cloud about the tree of the apparitions, and a loud noise at the Lady's departure.[1]

It is also remarkable that the children were shown a vision of hell that terrified them, and were given a specific prophecy announcing more *apparitions of unknown lights* in the sky:

> The war is going to end, but if people do not stop offending God another and worse one will begin during the reign of Pius XI.[2] When you see a night illuminated by *an unknown light* know that this is the great sign that God is giving you that he is going to punish the world for its crimes by means of war, famine, and persecution of the Church and of the Holy Father.
>
> To prevent this I shall come to ask for the consecration of Russia. . . . If they heed my requests, Russia will be converted and there will be peace. If not, she will spread her errors throughout the world.

The mixture of seriousness and absurdity that we have already noted in several contactee stories is an unmistakable characteristic of this statement. We will find the same thing to be true in Lourdes, where the alleged Virgin Mary

1. Quoted from Joseph Pelletier, "The Sun Danced at Fatima," (Worcester, Mass.: Assumption College, 1952).
2. Pius XI died in 1939.

instructs the little Bernadette to perform meaningless actions.

The pattern of prophecy followed its course, and the humans were duped. On August 13 there were eighteen thousand people at the site of the apparitions. The children, however, were not present. They had been kidnapped and jailed by a local official who had decided to put an end to this "nonsense." In their absence, a clap of thunder was heard, followed by a bright flash. A small whitish cloud was forming around the tree. It hovered for a few minutes, then rose and melted away. The clouds in the sky had turned crimson red, and then changed to pink, yellow, and blue. "Colored light like a rainbow on the ground"; "clouds around the sun reflecting different colors on the people"—such are some of the terms the witnesses used to describe it.[3] The witnesses saw "falling flowers," the famous phenomenon of "angel hair" so consistently reported after the passage of a UFO, and sometimes interpreted as an ionization effect. One man, Manuel Pedro Marto, reported seeing clearly *a luminous globe spinning through the clouds* ("Uma especie de globo luminoso girando nas nuvens") in a statement made under oath during the canonical enquiry concerning the "signs" of August 13, 1917.

On August 19 the children had been released and were tending sheep near Aljustrel, when about 4 P.M. they noticed a sudden lowering of the temperature. The sun, they said, became yellowish; the colors of the rainbow once again filled the countryside, visible to adults in the vicinity (as was later established). The bright flash was seen, and a glowing light came to settle about a tree near the children. The entity, clothed in white and gold, stood once more in the center of the glow. The witnesses fell on their knees and "feasted their souls in rapture." A dialogue fol-

3. Father Thomas McGlynn, *Vision of Fatima* (Boston: Little Brown & Co., 1968), pp. 44, 49.

lowed in which the apparition asked the children to "make sacrifices for sinners." After ten minutes the Lady of Light departed slowly toward the east with a roaring sound!

Apparitions of a Flying Globe

On September 13 the crowd numbered thirty thousand, including two "men in black" (wearing the distinctive Roman collar). These two priests were absolutely skeptical and had come specifically to establish the falsity of the much-heralded "miracles." The site of the apparitions was a wide amphitheater where most of the crowd had gathered to be close to the tree of the apparitions. However, the two skeptical priests had chosen a spot on the higher ground from which they could observe everything. The following is based on their report.

Noon. The sun got dimmer, although no clouds were seen in the sky. Thousands cried: "There She is . . . look!" A globe of light was seen by all, advancing slowly down the valley, from east to west, toward the children. It came to rest on the tree. A white cloud formed and out of the empty sky, shiny white "petals" began to fall. Let us ponder this description of the phenomenon by a witness:

> As the people stare at this strange sight they soon notice that the falling, glistening globules, contrary to the laws of perspective, grow smaller and smaller as they near them. And when they reach out their hands and hats to catch them they find that they have somehow melted away.

The children saw the entity again in the center of the globe, and the dialogue began once more between the Lady and Lucia. The promise of a miracle on October 13 was repeated. Then the radiant globe rose and disappeared *into the sun.*

Asked what he thought the globe was, one of the priests,

now quite shaken, stated that "it was a heavenly vehicle that carried the Mother of God from her throne above to this forbidden wasteland." The concept of the earth as a prison or a "forbidden wasteland" is decidedly a popular one among those who have been exposed to these phenomena.

The last apparition, as predicted, took place on October 13, 1917. The crowd numbered seventy thousand this time. (The size of the assembled crowd had grown in the following progression: 3, 50, 4,500, 18,000, 30,000, 70,000.) The vision was preceded by a flash of light at noon, a sweet strange fragrance. The children engaged in a dialogue with the Lady. The crowd did not hear the conversation and saw no Lady. They did observe the dramatic change on the faces of the three children, enraptured by the vision.

The predicted miracle took place as the apparition left the Cova da Iria. The rain, that had been pouring down on the crowd, suddenly stopped, and the heavy clouds parted. The sun appeared as a disk of brilliant silver, "a weird disk that turns rapidly on its own axis and casts off beams of colored lights in all directions. Shafts of red light shot out from the rim of the sun and colored the clouds, the earth, the trees, the people; then shafts of violet, of blue, of yellow and of other colors followed in succession." [4] These colors have been described as "monochromatic sectors" and they were definitely revolving.

The reports speak of a *flat disk* rather than a globe. After a while it stopped spinning and "plunged downward in zigzag fashion toward the earth and the horrified spectators."

Most witnesses believed that their last hour had come! Many of them began publicly confessing their sins. Finally the disk reverted its motion and disappeared into the sun, the real sun, once again fixed and dazzling in the sky. The

4. Pelletier, *op. cit.*, p. 123.

astounded crowd suddenly realized that their clothes, the trees, and the ground were perfectly dry.

Such is the story of Fatima as it can be reconstructed from reports of the time and from Church investigations. The final "miracle" had come at the culmination of a precise series of apparitions combined with contacts and messages that place it very clearly, in my opinion, in the perspective of UFO phenomena. Not only was a flying disk or globe consistently involved, but its motion, its falling-leaf trajectory, its light effects, the thunderclaps, the buzzing sounds, the strange fragrance, the fall of "angel hair" that dissolves upon reaching the ground, the heat wave associated with the close approach of the disk, *all of these are constant parameters of UFO sightings everywhere.* And so are the paralysis, the amnesia, the conversions, and the healings.

The Angel of Peace

Few of the books on Fatima provide us with details of the children's background. Yet in all apparition phenomena, it is crucial to investigate this background thoroughly and to ask as precisely as possible for descriptions of the earliest incidents which set the witness on a path to extraordinary realities. In the case of Fatima *the events did not begin*—as most authorities indicate—on May 13, 1917. It is true that such is the date of the first apparition of the Lady, but it had been preceded by a series of sightings of an angel a couple of years before.

In April, 1915, when Lucia was 8, she was reciting the rosary near Fatima when she saw a transparent white cloud and a human form. This happened a second time in the same year, and a third time in October. Then during 1916, Lucia was visited *three times* by the angel.

The first occasion was in the spring. Lucia was with two of her cousins when rain started to fall. The children sought shelter in a small cave. After lunch the rain had stopped and they were playing at the entrance of the cave when they heard the rumble of a powerful wind—another constant in UFO behavior—and a white light appeared. It was gliding through the valley above the tree tops. In the light was a youth of admirable beauty who came close to them and said: "I am the Angel of Peace".

He taught the children a prayer and left. The three little ones were left in a trance: they kept repeating and repeating the prayer, mechanically, until they literally fell from exhaustion.

The next incident took place on a hot day in midsummer 1916. This time, the angel appeared suddenly and asked:

"What are you doing? Pray! Pray a great deal! Offer prayers and sacrifices continually."

"How are we to offer sacrifices?" asked Lucia.

"Make a sacrifice of everything that you possibly can. . . . Above all, accept and bear with submission the suffering that the Lord shall send you."

The children were left paralyzed. It was only toward the evening that they regained their senses and began to play again. In this case, as in the previous one, the witnesses did not want to discuss the matter—not even among themselves.

> The experience has been so intimate and so manifestly sacred that none of them ever thinks of revealing it, or even the smallest part of it, to anyone else. It is obviously a favor to be kept for themselves. Of that they are absolutely and instinctively persuaded.[5]

The next day they still could not explain their reactions to the apparition: "I don't know what is happening to me," said one of the little girls. "I cannot speak, nor play, nor sing, and I haven't the strength to do anything." The angel appeared one more time, in the fall of 1916, in the cave at

---

5. Pelletier, *op. cit.*, p. 4. (This statement is one of the best definitions one could give for my strangeness category 6.)

Cabeso. He gave the children Communion. Analyzing the power that prompted the young witnesses to imitate the actions of this "angel" and to repeat his prayers slavishly, Pelletier offers this perceptive remark:

> This power is so intense that it absorbs and almost completely annihilates them. It practically deprives them of the use of their bodily senses . . . their bodies are subject to a mysterious, depressing force that prostrates them.

His remark could apply to the entire spectrum of close encounters with UFOs.

The Impact of Fatima

What were the sequels to the Fatima story? The lives of many people who attended the "miracles" were deeply changed. Some were cured of a variety of diseases.

> At my mother's request, I went once more to Cova da Iria in August at the time of the apparitions, writes engineer Mario Godinho. Once more I came back discouraged and disappointed. But that time, something extraordinary happened. My mother, who had had a large tumor in one of her eyes for many years, *was cured.* The doctors who had attended her said they could not explain such a cure.

This is just one among hundreds of such testimonies. At the time of the final miracle, many people were driven out of their senses, even those who saw it from a distance of several miles, and were not in the company of other witnesses who might have influenced them. A child of 12, named Albano Barros, for example, who was in a field near Minde, eight miles from Fatima, was so struck when he saw the disk of light falling toward the earth that *he does not remember what followed:* "I cannot even remember whether I took the sheep home, whether I ran, or what I

did." (In 1960 he had become a successful building con-
tractor in Somerville, New Jersey.) Others were so af-
flicted that, like farmer Manuel Francisco, they went home
weeping. Another witness, a lady who now lives in the
United States, near Albany, added this comment, "Even
today, whenever there is lightning, I remember it and I am
afraid." A prominent lawyer, Mr. Mendes, stated in an interview with John Haffert in 1960:

> What I saw at Fatima could not help but affect the inte-
> rior life and I am sure that all who saw the miracle, or
> even heard about it, cannot fail to be impressed by its
> greatness. . . . I still remember it today as vividly as at
> the moment it happened, and I feel myself to be domi-
> nated by that extraordinary event.[6]

Another witness reports: "I always keep thinking about
the sign." An extremely interesting series of testimonies
came from witnesses who were not at Cova da Iria, but
many miles away from the crowd. I have already mentioned the observation made by Albano Barros in Minde. A
woman named Mrs. Guilhermina Lopes da Silva, who
lived in Leiria no less than sixteen miles from the site of
the miracle, could not go to the place appointed for the apparition, but she looked toward the mountain at noon and
saw "a great red flash" in the sky. The brilliance in the sky
was such that it was seen thirty miles away (at San Pedro
de Muel, by Portuguese writer Afonso Vieira, his wife, and
his mother-in-law). The phenomenon, it seems, could not
be photographed directly with the photographic emulsions
and shutter speeds commonly available at the time. (One
picture often produced by the newspapers and alleged to
show the miracle is in fact a photograph of an eclipse of
the sun that has nothing to do with the Fatima miracle.)
There are many pictures of the crowd during the "mira-

6. John Haffert, *Meet the Witnesses* (Washington, N.J.: AMI Press,
1961), p. 78.

cle," however, and the actual brightness of the disk is an unresolved question. Two witnesses looked at it with binoculars and reported seeing a ladder and two entities. The edges of the disk, according to all descriptions, were sharp. And it was definitely not blinding, although pictures of the crowd show many witnesses shading their eyes. But others report that the phenomenon darkened the sun to such an extent that at one point they could see the moon and the stars.

Another remote witness was a schoolboy who was so impressed by what he saw that he subsequently became a priest. (John Haffert interviewed him in 1960.) At the time of the miracle he was with his brother and other children in the village of Alburitel, nine miles away from the Cova da Iria, and here is what he experienced:

> I looked fixedly at the sun which seemed pale and did not hurt my eyes. Looking like a ball of snow, revolving on itself, it suddenly seemed to come down in a zig-zag, menacing the earth. Terrified, I ran and hid myself among the people, who were weeping and expecting the end of the world at any moment. It was a crowd which had gathered outside our local village school and we had all left classes and run into the streets because of the cries and surprised shouts of men and women who were in the street in front of the school when the miracle began.
>
> There was an unbeliever there who had spent the morning mocking the "simpletons" who had gone off to Fatima just to see an ordinary girl. He now seemed paralyzed, his eyes fixed on the sun. He began to tremble from head to foot, and lifting up his arms, fell on his knees in the mud, crying out to God.
>
> But meanwhile the people continued to cry out and to weep, asking God to pardon their sins. We all ran to the two chapels in the village, which were soon filled to overflowing. During those long moments of the solar prodigy, objects around us turned all colors of the rainbow. . . . When the people realized that the danger was over, there was an explosion of joy.

Two of the three children at Fatima died young, as the Lady had predicted, but Lucia lived secluded in a convent to an advanced age.

The Secret of Prophecy

A man whose word I trust received an interesting report from one of the Pope's secretaries, who introduced the highest men in the Church into the presence of John XXIII for the opening of the secret part of the Fatima prophecy in 1960. Although the solemn event took place behind closed doors, the secretary had the opportunity to see the cardinals as they left the Pope's office: they had a look of deep horror on their faces. He got up from behind his desk and tried to speak to one of them whom he knew intimately, but the prelate gently pushed him aside and walked on with the expression of someone who has seen a ghost.

What revelation could have so shaken these men? Perhaps it was the confrontation with the nature of a phenomenon that transcends our reality *and our highest beliefs*, transcends our concepts of reason and of faith, and whose very absurdity appears carefully designed to misguide our probing minds. For what purpose?

From a rationalistic point of view it would be desirable, of course, to work solely on the basis of data coming from scientists and technically trained observers. Much of the UFO phenomenon is indeed presented in detailed accounts giving physical data. Hence *it has a technological basis*. But we cannot ignore the fact that the emotions it generates in the witnesses are religious in nature and that the documented facts regarding the purest cases of "miracles" (like Fatima) very closely match the patterns observed in many UFO cases. This leads me to reiterate an earlier statement: We are faced with a *technology* that transcends the physical and is capable of manipulating our reality, generating a variety of altered states of consciousness and of emotional perceptions. The purpose of that technology may be to change our concepts of the universe.

We must analyze carefully the morphology of miracles as we would analyze moon rocks, or a newly discovered species of insects. We must cynically take apart the testimonies, look into motives and fallacies, and isolate the underlying facts. Only then can we be equipped to discuss the implications.

The Physics of the B.V.M.

Thus far in this chapter we have examined one series of apparently miraculous events, namely those related to the Fatima observations of B.V.M., the entity described by percipients as the "Blessed Virgin Mary." These percipients, of course, have been exposed to such a powerful alteration of reality that their statements, from the observation on, are distorted by their emotions. This does not mean that we should reject their testimony. In the sixteenth century, people in great crowds fell on their knees and confessed their sins when they saw a comet. In many civilizations, eclipses produced the same effects. People behave in abject submission whenever presented with a potentially threatening cause that lies beyond their comprehension, a fact well known to those who have studied the human mind. The B.V.M. may dress in golden robes and smile radiantly to children, but the technology which "she" uses is indistinguishable from that of gods and goddesses of other tongues and garb; it is also indistinguishable from the technology surrounding the UFO phenomenon.

On February 11, 1858, a 14-year-old girl named Bernadette Soubirous was gathering firewood by a narrow stream near Lourdes, in the South of France, when she heard "a great noise, like the sound of a storm." She looked around her but neither the trees nor the water were disturbed. Then she heard the sound again. In fear, she looked straight up and "lost all power of speech and thought."

From a nearby cave or grotto came a golden-colored cloud. Soon after came an entity, described as a beautiful Lady, who placed herself above a bush that was moving as if it were windy. (At Fatima there was a wind which "moved across the mountain without touching the trees." [7] The Lady consistently appeared in the top branches of a small tree, whose center shoots were found bent toward the east, as though tilted in that direction when the apparition departed. Lucia, of Fatima, was closely questioned on this point and stated that "our Lady's feet rested lightly on the top of the leaves.") [8] Montes de Oca adds in his book *More About Fatima* that "the topmost branches of the tree were bent in the form of a parasol and remained thus as if an invisible weight had come to rest upon them." [9]

When the Lady of Lourdes looked at Bernadette, ALL FEAR LEFT HER, but she seemed TO KNOW NO LONGER WHERE SHE WAS. She wanted to pray but as she tried to lift her hand to her forehead *her arm remained paralyzed,* and it is only after the Lady had crossed herself that she could do the same.[10] When the story became known it was met with incredulity by the local authorities and by the priests. Father Peyramalle, who was the *curé* of the town, was especially angry and suggested that the Lady should make the rosebush bloom before the whole crowd in order to convince everyone. When Bernadette conveyed to the Lady this demand on the part of the local priest, the apparition simply smiled. For fifteen days she appeared to Bernadette, and their conversations centered on the Lady's request for a chapel and for processions

7. Haffert, *op. cit.,* p. 70.
8. McGlynn, *op. cit.,* p. 64.
9. Montes de Oca, *More About Fatima* (Dublin: Gill & Son, 1960), p. 8.
10. Stephen Breen, *Recent Apparitions of the B.V.M.* (New York: Lumen Books, 1951), p. 43.

there. At times the dialogue was totally absurd, and it was absurd in the same sense as the conversations with "ufo-nauts" we have reviewed. On one occasion, the Lady told Bernadette to go and wash herself in a nonexistent spring, and in another she ordered her bluntly to "go and eat the grass that grows over there!"

A study of these events from the point of view of the esoteric tradition might be rewarding. Occult masters like Gurdjieff and Crowley were wont to send their disciples on insane errands, such as carrying stones to a mountaintop as a test of their devotion. The early story of Mary, and the miracles that surround her life, point to intriguing similarities with earlier deities, and in particular with the Egyptian goddess Isis. However, we are not concerned here with an interpretation of mythology but with an attempt to deal with reports of observations that seem to form extraordinary patterns. One such pattern is that of the cloud and the cave, a common thread between Fatima, Lourdes and other apparitions. In a description given in the *Apocrypha* we find the same pattern:

> They stood in the place of the cave: And behold a bright cloud overshadowing the cave. And the midwife said: My soul is magnified this day, because mine eyes have seen marvelous things: for salvation is born unto Israel. And immediately the cloud withdrew itself out of the cave, and great light appeared in the cave so that our eyes could not endure it. And by little and little that light withdrew itself until the young child appeared.

A superficial examination of the phenomena of Lourdes would seem to indicate that a rather simple girl (Bernadette was illiterate and spent most of her day repeating prayers while accomplishing some menial chores for her very poor parents) simply turned into a visionary and soon shared her insanity with increasingly large crowds. But the story deserves closer examination.

First, there is the matter of the spring. During the ninth

apparition of the Lady, Bernadette was instructed to "go and wash and drink in the spring." But there was no spring! Bernadette looked for a spring, found none, and in despair began to dig into the sand. Water appeared and filled the hole, turning the soil to mud. Bernadette tried to wash and only managed to smear her face with the mud. The crowd laughed at her, especially when she attempted to drink and later began to eat the grass. Bernadette had dug the hole "in a sort of stupor" but seems to have done so at just the right time and place for a spring to appear. Indeed, the next day *there was a clean little stream at the spot,* going gaily down the hill and into the Gave river. A blind man named Louis Bourriette bathed his eyes in the spring and regained his sight. A dying baby was restored to full health.

The attitude of the crowd changed.

The next phase of the apparitions was marked by a request for penance. Bernadette was instructed to "kiss the ground for the sinners." The girl, and all those in attendance, began kissing the ground as a gesture of humility. The gesture is indeed a moving one. It is interpreted by many as a sweeping social panacea, as, for example, Stephen Breen says:

> They were setting an example of prayer and humility which could save Europe if applied to the social problems of the time, which, after all, are only a collection of personal problems, in the final analysis.[11]

Many of us will disagree with this rather simplistic and superficial view of social problems, but the point made here is the illustration of a mechanism through which phenomena such as UFO sightings and contacts with paranormal entities *can play a role far beyond their local impact.* For France at the end of the nineteenth century, as for Portugal in 1917, the apparitions of the mysterious Lady were

11. Breen, *op. cit.,* p. 37.

in many respects social and political turning points, deeply influencing the collective psyche.

Another interesting observation concerns the nature of the state of trance experienced by Bernadette. One doctor had decided to expose her as a mental case and performed a fascinating experiment. This man, a Dr. Douzous, witnessed a candle flame applied to Bernadette's hand for fifteen minutes, measured by his watch. When she finished her prayers he could observe the glow of ecstasy leaving her face.

> I asked her to show me her left hand. I examined it most carefully, but could not find the least trace of burning anywhere on it. I then asked the person who was holding the candle to light it again and give it to me. I put it several times in succession under Bernadette's left hand but she drew it away quickly, saying, "You're burning me." I record this fact just as I have seen it, without attempting to explain it.

Healing Phenomena

A final fact of interest concerns the healings that have occurred—and apparently continue to occur—in connection with the apparitions at Lourdes. I realize that a wide range of diseases do have psychosomatic causes (in other words, these diseases have a mental rather than a physical origin) and that suggestion, self-hypnosis, or faith will produce the appearance of amazing cures simply by removing the mental need for the illness. This is true of some types of paralysis, amnesia, blindness, etc. The cures performed at Lourdes, however, are not limited to such illnesses but extend to such improbable cures as tumors and broken bones!

In one celebrated example, a Belgian man named Pierre de Rudder had suffered a crushing blow to his leg from a falling tree. He had a compound fracture and the member became infected, but he refused amputation. The victim was almost unable to move, even with the help of crutches. A devout Catholic, he had no funds to travel to Lourdes itself, but was able to convince his employer to pay for his trip to the shrine of Our Lady of Lourdes in Oostacker, Belgium. The date for the pilgrimage was picked as April 7, 1875.

To understand what happened to de Rudder it is important to know the details of his medical record. A surgeon, Dr. Affenaer, had had to remove a piece of bone that had broken away and had inserted itself in the tissues. The bones were thus separated by a space of over one inch, and the patient had endured endless suffering during the *eight years* that had elapsed since the accident. De Rudder had seen many doctors, all of whom stated that nothing could be done, short of an amputation, to relieve the pain. Healing the broken bones was naturally out of the question. In January, 1875, another specialist, Dr. Van Hoestenberghe, had seen the patient and stated:

> Rudder had an open wound at the top of the leg. In this wound one could see the two bones separated by a distance of three centimeters. There was no sign of healing. Pierre was in great pain and suffered thus since eight years before. The lower part of the leg could be moved in all directions. The heel could be lifted in such a way as to fold the leg in the middle. It could be twisted, with the heel in front and the toes in back, all these movements being only restricted by the soft tissues.

Another doctor named Verriest confirmed this statement. Nine days before the pilgrimage the wound was observed by one Jean Houtsaeghe. He saw the ends of the two bones and confirmed that Pierre had another wound on the top of his foot. Several other witnesses saw the state of his leg as he changed his bandages. All were struck by the fact that the wound was in very poor condition. A detailed description is probably unnecessary.

Given the primitive state of hygiene at the time (Lister

had discovered antiseptics that very year, but his techniques were not yet in wide use) it is safe to say that Rudder was in deplorable condition. When he started his journey he spent two hours to reach the train station, walking the mile and a half distance with the help of his wife, using two crutches. A railroad employee named Bloome carried him into the train, but when he saw how his leg was swaying helplessly he couldn't help but saying: "What are you going to Oostacker for, in such a state as yours? Why don't you stay home instead?"

"Others have been cured in Oostacker," said Rudder. "So why not me?"

Finally they reached the little cave, where the people had erected a statute of Our Lady of Lourdes. Rudder sat down, but the crowd was such around him that his leg was repeatedly hit by passers-by, causing him great pain. He had tried to walk around the cave, like the other pilgrims, but after doing so twice he had to give up and sat down in exhaustion. He prayed. He begged to be allowed to work again, so that he could support his wife and children, and could stop relying on the charitable gifts of others. He felt deeply moved, overwhelmed by a strange feeling. Beside himself, he rose, *went through the crowd, and knelt before the statue. . . .* Then he suddenly realized what he had done! In joy, he began walking around the cave, and his wife saw him thus: "What happened?" she asked. "What are you doing? What are you doing?" She looked troubled, became dizzy, and fainted on the spot.

Rudder was immediately taken to a nearby house and his leg was examined. Not only was the wound neatly closed, but the leg had become completely normal again. The bones were no longer broken. *Both legs were of equal length.* Rudder was walking normally, and only experienced slight discomfort in wearing shoes again. When he arrived home, surrounded by the crowd like a national hero, his daughter threw herself into his arms, in tears. But his younger son, who had never seen him without his crutches, could not believe that this man was actually his father.

As soon as he heard of the case, Rudder's physician, Dr. Affenaer, rushed to his house. He was thus able to observe him the day following the cure, in the morning. He carefully examined the leg and was especially struck by the fact that the bones were perfectly smooth at the place where they had been broken. This examination was performed in the presence of several witnesses, who saw Dr. Affenaer break into tears and heard him say: "You are completely cured, de Rudder. Your leg is like that of a newborn baby."

Dr. Van Hoestenberghe also came to see his patient, but he did so only reluctantly because he refused to believe in any sort of miracle. He found Pierre working in his yard, digging. He was still incredulous and asked Rudder to submit to his examination. His patient, in a happy mood, jumped up and down before him to convince him he was really cured! The doctor found a scar just below the knee and another one on the foot. He also discovered that the bone was now unbroken and smooth throughout. Pierre was indeed walking normally.

Pierre de Rudder walked normally until his death from pneumonia, twenty-three years later, in 1898. During these twenty-three years he was an inspiration to all, and his experience brought many atheists back into the Church.

The story could have ended on the same note of speculative wonder that characterizes most accounts of paranormal events, had it not been for Dr. Van Hoestenberghe, a man of high intelligence and integrity, a genuine scientist who had become convinced of the reality of the "miracle" but had not allowed this belief to blind him when the documentation of the facts was concerned. Dr. Van Hoestenberghe asked and was granted permission to exhume the body and perform an autopsy on Pierre de Rudder. The operation was performed on May 24, 1899. The physician amputated both legs at the knee. The bones were examined and photographed. The pictures, which I have obtained, show with great clarity the deformation of the bones of the left leg. The healing has occurred in such a way, however, that the two legs are of equal length and the weight of the body can be equally supported. A fragment of bone is seen to be missing. The autopsy report was signed and published as part of a complete paper on the Rudder case, co-authored by Van Hoestenberghe, Deschamps, and Royer, in the *Revue des Questions Scientifiques*, in its issue of October, 1899. There is no explanation for the piece of healthy white bone, over one inch long, which connects the two sections still showing the traces of breakage. In their article the three doctors raise the hypothesis of faith-healing, that Charcot had formulated in connection with his analysis of several mental cases. The hypothesis, in their view, must be discounted.

They find it hard to admit that the nervous system, even in the most advanced cases of mental imbalance, could restore the destroyed tissues in violation of the known laws of natural healing of the body: "To state this [they say] is to place oneself in opposition to the principles of medical science." Several weeks are required for the healing of broken bones in the simplest cases. Instantaneous cure is out of the question. Yet de Rudder, like Dr. X (see Chapter One) was healed instantly. The technology of the B.V.M. and the technology of the UFO are once again seen to produce similar effects.

The Case of Guadalupe

I have in my library a copy of some unpublished notes by Evans-Wentz, one of the greatest students of folklore in this century. The ideas of this man have been of considerable interest to me because I owe to him some of the documentation in the study of the "Little People" I published in *Passport to Magonia*. Evans-Wentz, who knew equally well the popular traditions of Tibet and those of Scotland, had written in 1909 a dissertation in French, "Fairy-Faith in Celtic Countries," after traveling through Brittany, Ireland, Wales, and Scotland with local guides, gathering stories and tales from older men and women who had seen the "Good People." He knew nothing about our UFOs, of course, but an examination of the occupants of these strange machines led me to research historical analogues to their behavior, and I found such data, beautifully documented, in his work.

Evans-Wentz had been born in New Jersey but after all his life travels came to California and spent his last years near San Diego, where he befriended the local Indians and diligently studied their culture and traditions. He made some interesting discoveries in California and left many notes in manuscript form. They contain a theory that appears relevant in the context of this chapter on the relationship between religion and paranormal phenomena.

The section of Evans-Wentz' work of most interest here begins with some remarks about the Virgin of Guadalupe, to which I have already alluded earlier in this chapter. To him, the entity that appeared before a 57-year-old Indian named Juan Diego (his Nahuatl name was Singing Eagle) was not the Holy Virgin but the American goddess Tonantzin whom the Aztecs had adopted as the mother of all their other gods. The apparition took place on December 9, 1531, in Mexico. It began with the sweet sound of "singing birds," followed by a voice which came from the top of the hill. The source of the voice was hidden by "a frosty mist, a brightening cloud." The technology of the B.V.M. was at work!

When Juan Diego came to the top of the mountain he saw a radiantly beautiful young Mexican girl of about 14, standing in the light. A series of well-documented miracles followed, in which healings took place and mysterious flowers appeared. A basilica was built and immense crowds converted. (In the six years that followed the incident over eight million Indians were baptized.)

Here is a chronology of the miracle.

On Saturday, December 9, Juan Diego meets the entity and is told to run and instruct the Lord Bishop, in Mexico City, to build a chapel. (This is the same request made in Lourdes.) The Bishop thought Juan was insane.

On Sunday, December 10, Juan Diego went back to see the Bishop and impressed him with his sincerity. The prelate asked for a tangible sign, and Juan conveyed this answer to the Lady, who told him to come the next day.

On Monday, December 11, Juan Diego did not come, because his uncle was dying. He was unable to relieve his suffering and decided to get a priest the following day.

On Tuesday, December 12, the Indian ran across the mountain to get the priest, but was met and stopped by the apparition, who said:

> My little son, do not be distressed and afraid. Am I not here who am your mother? Are you not under my shadow and protection? Your uncle will not die at this time. This very moment his health is restored. There is no reason now for the errand you set out on, and you can peacefully attend to mine. Go up to the top of the hill. Cut the flowers that are growing there and bring them to me.

Singing Eagle knew well that there were no flowers on the top of the hill but to his surprise he found them there, cut them, and ran to the city to give them to the Bishop. When he arrived at the palace, unfortunately, the flowers dropped on the floor and he was much disappointed. To his great surprise the Bishop and all present suddenly knelt before him: upon his coarse garment, made of maguey fibers, had appeared the lovely image of an unearthly being, the figure of a woman, below her a crescent moon.

Evans-Wentz points out that December 12 was the ancient feast-day of the goddess Tonantzin, the dark-faced Earth-Mother, who thus remained the spiritual guardian of America in her modern guise as the Holy Virgin!

Other Shining Beings

The most interesting theory put forth by Evans-Wentz is a further development of his observation that ancient gods are continued under new names as the myths evolve from civilization to civilization, following the fortunes of war. Could it be, he asked, that every land has its own psychic and telluric forces, contributing to the appearance of certain spirit entities, regarded by human beings as gods and goddesses? Could the parallelism between Mormonism and ancient Indian beliefs be an example of such a mythological process?

Frank Waters had pointed out before Evans-Wentz that the early white settlers in America had become very closely Indian in spirit and feeling:

> They had confronted here that great psychic entity which was the spirit-of-place, the heart of a new continent. It shattered them completely. But each succumbed in a different way.[12]

The vision of God and Jesus experienced by Joseph Smith, the founder of the Church of Latter-Day Saints, was in fact, Evans-Wentz believes, a vision of the Shining Beings (known in other parts of the world as Devas). These Shining Beings appeared to Indians during special rituals which were kept very secret and were performed on high places or sacred mountains. Thus the Winnebagos tell of a youth who climbed the mountain, eager to find wisdom. He fasted for twelve days, and a spirit came to him, giving him knowledge and teaching him wonderful words, which brought health, welfare and long life. He came back to his people with a song expressing this newly discovered wisdom, and the song began:

> Into solitude went I
> And wisdom was revealed to me.

12. Frank Waters, *Masked Gods* (Albuquerque, N.M.: U. of New Mexico Press, 1950), p. 59.

> Saith the Spirit,
> Dream, oh, dream again,
> And tell of me,
> Dream thou!

Such a vision-quest is universal among the Indians of America, although among some races (such as the Pueblos and Navahos) it is limited to the priests and initiates. To Evans-Wentz, the beings contacted in the course of such visions are identical with the Celtic creatures of the Invisible Otherworld, and he concludes that there is evidence for their true existence. These beings are the guardians of secret places, "holding them in trust for a future of wonders." Evans-Wentz had been told by the Irish poet William Butler Yeats that such places existed and were thus guarded. He identifies one such spot in France, one in County Wicklow (Ireland), one in Campagna (Italy), and others in Asia and America.

Can we then use the vast and untapped reservoir of fantastic events in the collections of UFO lore to force an answer from our gods old and new, to bring them down to a human dimension, or to understand their power? Or do we find ourselves locked in their maze, their "fly bottle"? Is the time of our inquiry always wrong, the place always elsewhere? When we ponder the morphology of miracles or the poor, twisted bones of Rudder, are the angels in heaven rejoicing or do they laugh at our stupidity?

The Mormon Story

> I discovered a light appearing in my room, which continued to increase until the room was lighter than at noonday, when immediately a personage appeared at my bedside, standing in the air, for his feet did not touch the floor. . . .
>
> He called me by name, and said unto me that he was a messenger sent from the presence of God to me, and that his name was Moroni; that God had a work for me to do; and that my name should be had for good and evil among all nations, kindreds and tongues. . . .

Thus begins the account of the revelation of the Book of Mormon with the story of what transpired on the night of September 21, 1823, between Joseph Smith and an angel. The book itself, the angel stated, was in the form of gold plates that lay buried at a certain spot, and could be translated with the help of two stones in silver bows, that were buried with the plates.

> After this communication, I saw the light in the room begin to gather immediately around the person of him who had been speaking to me, and it continued to do so, until the room was again left dark, except just around him, when instantly I saw, as it were, a conduit open right up into heaven, and he ascended until he entirely disappeared.

In 1842, at the request of Colonel Wentworth of the *Chicago Democrat*, Joseph Smith wrote a sketch of the history of the Mormon Church that contained additional details on the apparition:

> On a sudden a light like that of day, only of a far purer and more glorious appearance and brightness, burst into the room; indeed the first sight was as though the house was filled with consuming fire. The appearance produced a shock that affected the whole body. In a moment a personage stood before me surrounded with a glory yet greater than that by which I was already surrounded. . . .
>
> I was told where there were deposited some plates, on which was engraved an abridgement of the records of the ancient peoples that had existed on this continent. The angel appeared to me three times the same night and unfolded the same things.

It is important to note that *this apparition was not Joseph's first vision.* Indeed he had "been forbidden to join any of the religious sects of the day" because he had claimed to have been favored by a mystical revelation while he was alone in the wilderness at the age of 14 (see below).

When Angel Moroni appeared to him he had been praying for a vision, for, he says, "I had full confidence in ob-
taining a divine manifestation, as I had previously had
one." [13] The angel appeared three times during the night
of September 21, 1823 (which happens to be the Autumn
Equinox), repeating exactly the same words. After the
third time Joseph was surprised to hear the cock crow and
to find that daylight was approaching, "so that our interviews must have occupied the whole of that night."

Joseph Smith got up and began his normal chores, but
he found himself so exhausted that he couldn't work in
any useful way. His father thought he was sick and told
him to go home, and on the way he fell to the ground
when trying to cross a fence, and remained unconscious.
The angel then appeared to him once more and told him to
repeat his words to his father, and to reveal his instructions. The father told Joseph to go and do as he had been
commanded, and that "these things were of God."

Thus the young man was allowed to go to the place
where the plates were buried, and he found them inside a
stone box which he had no difficulty opening, but he was
unable to take the plates out of the box. Again the angel
appeared, and told him to come back precisely in one year
and every year after that; four years later he would be permitted to take the plates.

The remainder of the story is well known. Thanks to the
help of a wealthy farmer named Martin Harris, Smith was
able to work on the translation of the golden plates, which
he read with the help of special stones he had found in the
box. When Harris took the plates and the beginning of the
translation to Professor Charles Anthon of New York, this
learned gentleman stated that the translation was correct,
"more so than any he had before seen translated from the
Egyptian." Looking at the plates that had not yet been
translated, he said that they were Egyptian, Chaldaic, As-

13. *Concerning the Origin of the Book of Mormon,* Source material by
Francis Kirkham (privately printed, 1937), p. 24.

syrian, and Arabic, and signed a statement to that effect
(which he later tore to pieces, however, when he learned
that the young man had found the plates upon the instructions of an angel!).

Eleven persons have stated that they saw the plates un-
earthed by Joseph Smith. In June, 1829, in response to a
communication obtained by Smith, the Mormon prophet
retired to the woods accompanied by Martin Harris, David
Whitmer, Oliver Cowdery, and knelt "in fervent prayer,"
hoping to receive a vision of the plates. As nothing happened, Martin Harris withdrew from the group, believing
that it was his presence that prevented the miracle from
taking place. The others resumed their prayers and, after a
few minutes, an angel stood before them, holding the
plates: "He turned over the leaves one by one, so that we
could see them and discern the engravings thereon distinctly." This can be usefully compared with the visions of
the young farmer of Aveyron.

The Book of Mormon was first published in 1830. It is a
strange document, similar in many ways to the OAHSPE
bible or the BOOK OF URANTIA, two accounts of early
history similarly "inspired" by divine intelligence.[14] In
1973 Jacques Bergier proposed to me an amusing explanation for the existence of these books which seem to ema-
nate from a cosmic source and, like the Bible, have come
to us through automatic writing or some other form of psychic revelation. There exists, he postulates, a civilization
in our galaxy which is broadcasting at regular intervals
some cosmic education program, much in the same manner as the French National Radio is every day broadcasting selected lectures in philosophy and history from the
Sorbonne. Just as the French are beaming these broadcasts
to Africa and other remote places, we could well visualize

14. The OAHSPE bible is an account of the origins and antiquity of
mankind and contains many references to the Red Men. It was received
psychically by John Ballou Newbrough about 1881, and it originated with
Shining Beings whom he calls "Angels."

an advanced civilization broadcasting very advanced concepts on psychic wavelengths, to be picked up by gifted prophets on earth and millions of other retarded planets!

Such differences as exist between the Koran, the Bible, the Book of Mormon and other sacred texts would be due to the imperfect understanding of the various individuals who pick up these broadcasts, just as four or five sorcerers from different African tribes, playing at night with old radio sets in different parts of the jungle, might obtain very different impressions of the civilized world through the Sorbonne cultural broadcasts . . . especially if they did not know what the Sorbonne was, and had only a limited acquaintance with the French language!

It is futile to engage in a debate concerning the truth or falsity of the statements made by Joseph Smith. We are looking here for indications of a higher order, and we can define as a miracle any event, real or imagined, or even faked, which creates certain paranormal, but verifiable effects. The transformation of an ordinary farmboy from rural New York State into an unchallenged leader of multitudes is, in my view, an unusual fact which deserves investigation. When we trace the turning point of this man's life to the sighting of a strange light and to contact with an entity inside the light, I believe the account needs to be preserved along with those we have already found in other faiths and other lands.

Let us return to Evans-Wentz' notes regarding Mormonism mentioned in my discussion of Shining Beings. Evans-Wentz was intrigued by Joseph Smith's first vision, which was not an apparition of Angel Moroni but of two entities whose names he was not privileged to learn. This took place during Smith's fifteenth year, as he was praying in a wood:

> I saw a pillar of light exactly over my head, above the brightness of the sun, which descended gradually until it fell upon me. . . . When the light rested on me I saw

two personages, whose brightness and glory defy all descriptions, standing above me in the air. One of them
spake unto me.[15]

As the translator of the Tibetan Book of the Dead, Evans-
Wentz recognized that the role played by Smith in bringing out the Book of Mormon was similar to that of the *Ter-
tons*, the "takers-out" of secreted scriptures in Tibet. However, the *Book of Mormon* claims to be the "sacred history
of ancient America." It states that the Indians are the rem-
nant of an Israelite tribe that settled in America six
hundred years before Christ. This is a difficult statement
to take seriously in the light of modern anthropology. Thus
we are again confronted with a mixture of certainty and absurdity, of fact and fantasy. We recognize here the third
coverup. Were such messages deliberately given to isolate
the believers from the society around them?

In an article published in the April, 1974, issue of *Occult* magazine, Jerome Clark and Loren Coleman point out
that the history of Mormonism contains many references to
three mysterious beings who might be three of Christ's
American Apostles, who asked to be allowed to remain on
earth until his Second Coming. The Three Nephites have
been seen several times since the days of Joseph Smith,
and form an interesting and colorful counterpart to the
Three Men in Black of modern UFO lore. These Nephites
are sometimes seen singly, and they perform miracles and
healings. In one of the stories quoted by Clark and Coleman, a Utah woman named Squires who was expecting the
return of her husband, and had seen no one around her
house while drawing water from the well a minute before,
suddenly found herself confronted with a gray-haired man
wearing a long white beard, who requested something to
eat and soon remarked that "she was not well." When she
acknowledged that indeed she was suffering from a pain

15. *The Pearl of Great Price*, part of the sacred Mormon text, published
as *The Triple Combination*.

under her shoulder, the unknown man replied: "God bless you, Sister. You will never want for anything again. You will always be blessed with plenty." He walked out the door, but when Mrs. Squires followed him outside he had vanished, and she could not see where he had gone! The date of the incident is given as the summer of 1874. Her health and money problems disappeared soon after, and she lived to the age of 89.

A Unified Theory of Apparitions

In many UFO stories of the olden days the witnesses thought they had seen angels from God and for this reason never bothered to report their experiences. Others thought they had seen devils. The difference may be very small. Commenting on the childhood experiences of Cayce and Geller, a British researcher named Peter Rogerson has reminded me that similar stories were common in accounts of mediums of various kinds:

> Andrew Jackson Davis, "The Poughkeepsie Seer," claimed to have met a mystical personage who gave him a staff in which there were little boxes which gave "cures to various diseases." The account follows the classical pattern of the evolution of the shaman. Mircea Eliade in his book *Shamanism* records the words of various shamans and how they became aware of the shamanistic powers. Accounts are often of the nature "I was washing by the river when a great ball of fire came down from the sky, it entered me, then I knew I was to become a shaman." [16]

Since the publication of *Passport to Magonia* I have received many interesting letters. "Until now I thought I had seen a messenger from Heaven," writes one witness. "I understand, having read your book, that I had witnessed a UFO." Some of the stories are strange yet consistent enough to become the nucleus of a new religious

16. Private communication from Peter Rogerson.

movement if the witness were of the proper psychological inclination. Perhaps only one close encounter in ten thousand starts a new faith, a new sect, or a new belief. When the right combination of social and psychological conditions is met, when the phenomenon finds a witness a ready believer, then revelation takes place.

Everything works as if the revelation were designed to isolate the witness, prophet, or believer from his social environment. He becomes an outcast and has to flee. This has been the fate of at least two police officers and of numerous other UFO witnesses. In France, several farmers saw their fields nearly ruined. The man in Michigan who reported the Swamp Gas case was jeered at in the streets and people came in cars to throw bottles at his house.

The believers, if they seek a climate in which to pursue their new life in accordance with the implications of their vision, have to create their own sect and move away. Moses did this. So did Joseph Smith. Often one sees the leader deserted by his wife and family. The spouse is especially likely to feel rejected and to betray him at the time when he most needs comfort. The wife of Martin Harris burned 116 newly translated pages of the Book of Mormon. The wives of several policemen involved in UFO incidents divorced them.

Sometimes the specific instructions given to the believers are such that their group continues to be persecuted for centuries (Jews) and have to endure great hardships before finding a place where they can settle down (Israel, Utah). The leaders are harassed by crowds (in one town the police chief's own trailer was destroyed by fire, blamed on arson) and often put to death (Jesus was crucified, Joseph Smith was lynched by a crowd in Illinois).

I think the stage is set for the appearance of new faiths, centered on the UFO belief. To a greater degree than all the phenomena modern science is confronting, the UFO can inspire awe, the sense of the smallness of man, and an idea of the possibility of contact with the cosmic. The religions we have briefly surveyed began with the miraculous experiences of one person, but today there are thousands for whom the belief in otherworldly contact is based on intimate conviction, drawn from what they regard as personal contact with UFOs and their occupants. The phenomenon and its effects are working here as they have worked at Fatima and Lourdes and in other places.

Table 2 should make this clear. The first column summarizes the physical effects described by witnesses of the miracles we have reviewed, in the actual words of the persons who reported them. The second column contains descriptions of the state of the persons contacted by UFOs, both during and after the experience. I think the reader can draw his or her own conclusions. I invite you to seek other documents in any library to complete this morphology of miracles with fresh material. You need not fear any paucity of data.

TABLE 2

Religious Miracles	UFO Events
"A frosty mist, a brightening cloud"	"They saw a light spreading around them like a mist"
Guadaloupe, December 9, 1531	*Magonia*, case 402 *
"A shock that affected the whole body"	"He was found unconscious"
"loss of sense of time"	"fainting, amnesia and return to the site in a trancelike state"
"so exhausted he couldn't move"	*Magonia*, case 482
	"he felt pricklings throughout his body, had to stop, lost his balance several times"
"fell to the ground and remained unconscious"	
Smith, September 21, 1823	*Magonia*, case 102

Religious Miracles	UFO Events
"a pillar of light which descended"	"he found a strong light beam aimed at him"
"a conduit right up to Heaven"	"he had no recollection of starting the car again"
"a light appearing in the room"	*Magonia*, case 893
Joseph Smith, the Book of Mormon, 1820 and 1823	"a vertical beam of light was aimed at him, disappeared with a flash"
	Magonia, case 921
"a golden colored cloud"	"the object went up into a cloud of unusual color, which flew against the wind"
"a great noise like the sound of a storm"	*Magonia*, case 575
Lourdes, February 11, 1858	"took off with a rush of air that rocked the car"
	Magonia, case 81
"lost all power of speech and thought"	"he fell unconscious as a vivid light enveloped him. He was unable to move his left arm
"knew not where she was"	for three days, and suffered from pain and extreme
"her arm was paralyzed"	nervousness"
Lourdes, February 11, 1858	*Magonia*, case 912
"left in a trance"	"the witness felt so weak all of a sudden that he had to drop
"fell from exhaustion"	the gun"
Fatima, spring 1916	*Magonia*, case 339

TABLE 2 *(Continued)*

Religious Miracles	UFO Events
"a transparent white cloud" "white light gliding above the tree-tops"	"they saw a large source of light in mid-air and heard piercing whistling sounds" *Magonia*, case 870
"rumble of a powerful wind" Fatima, April, 1915, and spring 1916	"it took off with a swooshing sound" *Magonia*, case 77
"the power annihilates them" "deprives them of the use of their bodily senses" "no strength the next day" Fatima, summer 1916	"the boy arrived home like a madman. The horse and the dog were paralyzed for several minutes" *Magonia*, case 916 "he found himself paralyzed and observed that birds had stopped singing and that cows seemed unable to move" *Magonia*, case 82
"a glowing light almost blinded them" "a bright flash" Fatima, May 13, 1917	"the witness was suddenly engulfed in a bluish-white light so dazzling he had to stop" *Magonia*, case 870
"a cloud rose from the vicinity of the tree" "tree branches were bent" "an explosion" Fatima, June 13, 1917	"An unusual noise, a whirlwind of flames coming towards the vineyard" "plants moved violently" "it flew south with a deafening roar" *Magonia*, case 391

Religious Miracles	UFO Events
"a buzzing or humming sound"	"it moved slowly, producing a humming sound and illuminating their car"
"a loud noise"	
	Magonia, case 425
Fatima, July 13, 1917	
"a small whitish cloud forms"	"a flattened dome giving off a blinding light, illuminating the countryside"
"falling flower petals, melt away"	
"a luminous globe spinning through the clouds"	"it flew away while a bright cloud slowly fell to the ground at the site"
"a bright flash"	*Magonia*, case 255
Fatima, August 13, 1917	
"glowing light settles about a tree"	"a silvery disk maneuvering in the sky"
"a strange fragrance"	"a feeling of intense cold"
"lowering of temperature"	*Magonia*, case 537
"bright flash," "roar of a rocket"	"a powerful odor as the object left"
Fatima, August 19, 1917	*Magonia*, case 615
"a globe of light advancing along the valley"	"they heard a strange numming sound and saw two disks hovering 1 m. above the ground"
"comes from E to W and rests on tree"	
"a white cloud forms"	"they rose with a sharp whistling sound, while trees below them bent double"
"shiny white petals fall"	*Magonia*, case 442
Fatima, September 13, 1917	

TABLE 2 (*Continued*)

Religious Miracles	UFO Events
"a weird disk that turns rapidly"	"A disk three times as large as the sun, red and purple, spinning rapidly, was seen descending swiftly toward the ground"
"a flat disk plunges in zig-zag fashion"	
"the clothes of the witnesses were dry in spite of the recent rain"	*Magonia,* case 321
Fatima, October 13, 1917	"When the object left, a cloud of dense smoke was forming under the rain. The witness found the trees, grass and ground perfectly dry"
	Magonia, case 292

* "Magonia" refers to *Passport to Magonia* by Jacques Vallee (Chicago: Regnery, 1969). The case numbers are those of the corresponding sighting summaries in the appendix entitled "A Century of UFO Landings."

CHAPTER EIGHT

Who Are You, Mr. Geller?

When Spirits begin to speak with a man, he must beware
that he believe nothing that they say. For nearly everything they say is fabricated by them, and they lie: for if
they are permitted to narrate anything, as what heaven is
and how things in the heavens are to be understood,
they would tell so many lies that a man would be as-
tonished.

—Swedish mystic Emanuel Swedenborg,
eighteenth century

Spirits have recently spoken with human beings. Not in
faraway places, mind you, but right in New York, and in
California, and in Washington, D.C. And people have ignored Swedenborg's warnings, and believed what they
said. In a particularly remarkable case, the communication
has given rise to what appear to be spectacular violations
of physical laws by a young Israeli named Uri Geller. Are
these claims of strange powers real? And how are they
related to the quiet pursuits of the Invisible College?

A Personal Appraisal of Uri Geller

Uri Geller asked the subject to select a three-digit number
and to write it down on the board. As he gave these instructions a number came into my consciousness and I

noted it on the pad I was using to keep a record of the experiments, showing it to Janine as I did so. The number I wrote was 726. The subject wrote a number on the board: the digits were 7, 2, and 5. Geller was sitting in a corner at the other end of the room, his head turned toward the wall and hidden by a screen. He spelled out the digits he said he was mentally picking up: 7, 2, and 5.

Here was a little puzzle. The Parapsychology Research Group of Palo Alto, of which I am one of the directors, had performed such experiments before. I had found most of them inconclusive. Clearly a clever stage magician could duplicate such mind-reading. It appeared to me, on the other hand, that in a small number of cases evidence did exist for extrasensory transfer of information between brains. While most researchers theorize about a process of transmission (similar to the transmission of an electromagnetic signal) in an effort to explain such phenomena, I am more inclined to think in terms of a *convergence of events.* Usually only two events converge: person A picks a number and person B picks the same number, which is then interpreted as person B guessing the number picked by A. In our little puzzle with Uri Geller, the interesting fact was the third element. Why had I written down 726 on my piece of paper before the subject had written anything on the blackboard?

Uri Geller appears capable of forcing subjects to pick certain numbers or certain words. This ability complicates the task of sorting out the observations. Writing a word on a card which the subject does not see, Geller would ask the person to think of the capital of a country. Then the subject suddenly realizes that he has forgotten the name of the capital of Great Britain, France, or the United States! The only name in his mind is a strange-sounding word that he does not recognize, but offers anyway as a last resort. Uri triumphantly turns over the card where he has written precisely *that same name,* which happens to be the capital of some country in Latin America! Knowing about this ability, I asked Uri privately if he had played a similar game with his subject on the night of the experiment, and he assured me that he had not. In other words, if we accept his word that he had not selected the number 725 in advance, then we are left with the theory that somehow, in our universe of events, there were three things that converged: the writing of the digits on the board, the guessing (if it was guessing) of these digits by Uri, and my recording of an almost identical number on my notebook prior to all this.

As we have seen before in Chapter Two, the events around Geller include contact with what he and Puharich have described as UFO entities.

Uri Geller came to the U.S. about 1970 at the request of Dr. Andrija Puharich, who was well-known among psychic phenomena research circles and could therefore expose him quickly to a significant audience. Of special interest was Uri's psychokinetic ability. (The word psychokinesis has been given to the ability to move objects at a distance without touching them, a feat that traditionally has been regarded as one of the tests of the miraculous.) In the case of Geller, not only is this ability claimed, but it apparently includes the faculty of distorting metal objects and even partly or completely dematerializing them. If demonstrated in the laboratory, such a phenomenon would be of great import to physics, but at the time of this writing no demonstration of this ability has been provided in strict laboratory control environments, although a wealth of anecdotal evidence is available.

One further interesting aspect of Geller's gift is that he *does not control it.* Instead, the effects happen more or less spontaneously in his vicinity. They are not under control of his intelligence, but of a form of volition of the same order as that responsible for the communications with AFFA or with 7171. In the communications channeled through Geller the source of this power has identified itself as emanating from UFOs.

Telepathy Experiments

Some of the scientists I know are very excited about Geller and expect breakthroughs to arise out of his work. Others assure me that he is definitely using trickery in all of his demonstrations. I am inclined to believe that although Geller, like every medium, uses trickery at times, some of the phenomena that happen around him are genuine. At the meeting of the Parapsychology Research Group mentioned earlier Geller did not demonstrate metal bending to anyone's satisfaction, and many members went away with grave doubts. But my own continued interest in Geller's work arose from different observations—specifically from two personal occurrences that I could not account for in terms of stage magic.

In December, 1972, I had lunch with Geller and showed him the series of Phoenician seals described in Chapter Six. They depict a religious ritual performed by priests, and a flying disk from which God-like creatures are emerging. Uri studied these photographs with much interest and proceeded to tell me confidentially the details of his own close encounters with UFOs. He was in fact, I learned, a "secret contactee," a man who believed himself to be in contact with an alien entity which he did not want to mention in public. A year and a half later this information was revealed by Puharich and others in a series of articles and books, and it has been a part of the UFO literature ever since. Yet all the alleged evidence that these articles and books contain has only deepened the problem instead of clarifying it. The central question remains to determine whether or not Uri is being used by something that wants to *appear* as a higher entity.

During our discussion I asked Uri Geller if he thought he could contact the UFO entity again to obtain for us a real test case: a close observation of a flying saucer. He replied that in all his meetings with "them" the initiative for the contact has been with the "other side."

Later during our lunch Uri proposed to do telepathic experiments with me. It is this short series of tests that convinced me that his abilities were genuine. The very first test in the series contained an unusual aspect that precluded trickery. One of the physicists with whom Geller had been working handed me a sealed envelope containing a card on which a target had been drawn. It was the outline of a whale blowing water vapor into the air. I "sent" it to Uri by visualizing the drawing on a television-like screen which I scanned slowly, erasing it mentally as I did so. Uri was to imagine a similar screen in his own mind and fill out the picture, but he received no clear image at the first trial. We decided to start again, and this time my attention fell on a fountain which was clearly visible behind Uri, in the courtyard of the building. The fountain reminded me of the water thrown into the air by the whale. I filled my mental television screen with the fountain, and sent that. Then I filled it with the form of a fish, and projected it a second time. Now Uri took a blank card and said, as he rapidly drew on it, "It's strange, I'm getting two things." On the card he passed around, he had drawn a fish. Next to the fish was a fountain. He thought it made no sense at all. This was a convincing test because it excluded the "collusion" hypothesis. I could not be absolutely sure that Uri had not managed to look into the envelope by trickery even before it was sealed that morning. But if he had done so he would have drawn a single target. I was the only person who knew that *two different targets*, rather than one, had been sent!

Mind over Matter

Now I began to take Uri Geller more seriously. In the second experiment he asked me to write a digit (I wrote down 8) and a second one (9) and then a third, larger. I wrote 2.

"Send me the last digit only," he said. And a moment later he had written a 2 on a card. This was not a com-

pletely foolproof case, because he might have spent long
and tedious hours training himself to read muscular motions at a distance and he could have guessed that I wrote
a 2 by observing the movement of my wrist. The interesting fact here was that my 2 was hastily drawn and that the
horizontal base of the digit was very flat and elongated. It
was completely different from the usual American way of
drawing it. Now the drawing by Uri was not only similar to
mine: it was *identical*, as was soon demonstrated by super-
imposing the two tracings. One was practically a carbon
copy of the other.

The discussion then came to the events that had taken
place at the Research Group meeting. Uri wanted to repeat
an experiment with colors. "Think of a color," he told me,
and immediately I thought "blue." Indeed I thought of
blue so suddenly that I assumed Uri had already selected
the answer and had somehow planted it in my mind. For
this reason, I deliberately changed my choice, reviewed a
dozen colors, and picked yellow as the target. Three times
Uri gave me the signal to send him the color. Then he
calmly announced:

"The color I receive is yellow, but once out of three
times I got the color blue."

By this time we had finished dessert and we had empty
ice cream cups before us.

"You know," said Uri, "everything you've seen . . .
Those are little things. This is not what I really do. My
specialty is to produce phenomena with physical objects.
For example, take a spoon."

With these words he touched, barely touched the spoon
in his cup, and he jumped back as if he had touched a
snake. He reached for the spoon again and showed it to us.
It was bent three times, literally folded back against the
handle. I took my own spoon and bent it with all my
strength against the edge of the table. There was no way I
could bend it to twist the wider part of it.

The Dangers of Blind Belief

Listening to Uri as he "explains" his power is very similar to reading those old records by a nineteenth-century medium describing the source of his knowledge. In both cases we are told that the power does not lie within the man himself, but emanates from one of two sources, either a higher spiritual center or a race of extraterrestrial beings. What are the consequences of taking such a statement at face value? We would have to assume that a higher intelligence is not only cognizant of our existence and development here on earth, but has decided to interfere with human affairs. Why would it choose to manifest itself through a man like Uri Geller, who is unashamedly seeking money and fame and delights in the confusion he throws his scientific supporters into every time he is "exposed" by someone claiming trickery? Are we necessarily dealing with the same phenomenon that is responsible for the sightings of unidentified flying objects? Couldn't we explain UFOs if we could explain Uri Geller?

Some scientists wonder whether Geller is not the latest in a series of artifacts released among the human race. Geller himself, it seems, would like us to believe that this is the case, and he encourages his followers to regard him as an emissary from a higher agency.

It is true that a change is taking place among scientists; a climate is being created in which it becomes permissible to hypothesize the existence of paranormal effects. There is probably much new knowledge to be gained in this direction. But there are also dangers in a rapid and uncritical shift in attitudes from skepticism to belief. By falling into either of the two extremes of secrecy and openness, of rejection and worship, we are decreasing our chances of finding the truth about Geller and about any unexplained phenomenon.

Building a Bridge

I have long had an interest in both UFO manifestations
and such psychic manifestations as telepathy, poltergeists,
and psychokinetics, but I have refrained (until a few years
ago) from attempting to build a bridge between these two
fields. To be sure, I have been aware that many UFO cases
contained elements indicative of psychic phenomena. At
the same time, I have found in the literature of psychic
history many observations that were suggestive of either
the presence or the interference of UFOs. It would have
been impossible not to recognize these connections and
yet, to give just one example, when I was recently invited
to speak about UFO research at a University of California
extension course on psychic phenomena, my decision to
accept the invitation was greeted with disbelief among astronomers privately interested in the subject. One of my
physicist friends who was studying the material aspect of
the sightings even called me to ask, "Why are you getting
such a solid field as UFO research mixed up with the dis-
reputable area of psychic phenomena?" implying that by
speaking of the analysis of UFO sightings before specialists in brain research, meditation, biofeedback, and brain-
wave analysis, I might jeopardize my chances of ever cap-
turing a real, material flying saucer!

At the same time, it was amusing to observe the initial
reluctance of those who had spent all their lives studying
poltergeists, telepathy, and the human aura to consider the
subject of UFOs.

But once the connection was established, there could
not be any more doubt that we had to deal with one, not
with two subjects; not with two sets of phenomena but
with a single universe of events in which a single set of
laws was in force.

It is no longer enough to ask "Who are *you*, Mr. Geller?"
We must also ask "Who are *we?*" And why is it at this
precise time in the history of our race that observations of

unusual events suddenly loom into our environment by the thousands? We have fought long and hard on this planet to establish a community of scientific thinkers governed by principles of rationality. People like Uri Geller—and that higher entity who he claims to be the source of his power—are now challenging the comfort of this community.

The changing attitudes of the public bear witness to the wider acceptance of nonrational events. I receive letters from people in many different positions, commenting on the relationship between UFOs and psychic phenomena. Some of these contain personal experiences that parallel those of Geller; sometimes they quote messages received from alleged superior entities similar to those Puharich claims to have contacted.

Experiences from Readers

"At the age of seven, I had a Sun experience similar to the Fatima case," writes one of my correspondents. "It occurred at sunset on the day of my father's funeral. . . . Your argument that UFO experiences exist through which both individuals and groups of people have been changed introduces the concept that understanding, like energy, may come in lumps, and may be quite different from that which results from preacher and school teacher proddings. . . ."

Another reader, a woman affiliated with a Fatima devotee group, expresses her belief that the Pilgrim Virgin may be nothing more than a point of psychic focus, "upon which that which is already in the devotee's unconscious is projecting."

One of my colleagues, an astronomer by training, is interested in a parallel between the phenomena described by Carlos Castaneda and those of UFOs. His letter throws an interesting light on the Geller case:

I read Castaneda's books on Don Juan and was struck by the rational absurdity of the experiences he reported. Of course, such properties are also characteristic of both UFO and ESP phenomena (and, at least in my experience, dreams as well). In UFOs we see violations of the laws of physics (instantaneous disappearances, quiet supersonic motion) and what seems to be a teasing manifestation in form somewhat ahead of its time, technically (i.e., the 1897 airships). In ESP and, I think UFOs, there seems to be manipulation of time as well as space. If we are dealing with what Castaneda calls a separate reality it is of interest not only to know what that reality is (is like) but how access from one reality to another is achieved. I regard it as a cultural artifact that only rational phenomena are respectable. I doubt that many people are sufficiently aware of the degree we are moulded by our culture and environment. In the past year *Science* magazine has reported two experiments along these lines. In the first, kittens were given a carefully controlled visual pattern for their first few days of vision, and the result was that they were subsequently able to perform good visual discrimination only against the same pattern. The visual cortex developed in response to the first patterns presented to it. In the second experiment it was shown that natives unfamiliar with large-scale rectilinear features (cities, highways and the like) were unable to interpret perspective in drawings.

Thus I feel our culture, education and training lead us to see the world in a certain way and, apparently, lead us to comfortably ignore or reject those aspects of reality that don't fit.

My correspondent goes on to describe a case of UFO-related psychic phenomena that he has himself investigated:

This person began experiencing ESP situations in his early teens. His first experiences were apparitions seen in his bedroom at night (also seen by other family members). Also an intense bluish-white light would occasionally materialize at the foot of his bed. Almost too bright to look at directly, its center was yellow. . . . At about this time he observed UFOs twice, both times with other boys. The first sighting was a night flyby of several greenish oval objects; a few days later similar objects were seen again and were thought to have landed in a nearby wood. Upon searching the woods, the next day the witness and his friends were resting in a clearing where they believed the UFO may have landed. Hearing a noise behind them they turned and saw a man watching them from behind a bush. Of average height, he was dressed in a tight-fitting blue jacket like a policeman might wear, but without metal buttons, badges or other decoration. . . . The figure didn't speak but just stared at them and in a moment the boys fled in fear.

In the next decade this man experienced spontaneous levitation twice and made several out-of-the-body trips, the longest being from his military base in Japan to the home of a friend in California (the friend saw him at the door of the room at the corresponding time).

Other letters come directly from witnesses, some of them regarding themselves as experienced in the paranormal field:

Four times I have received a telepathic "message" concerning UFOs. Not like a sound or voice. It was a sequence of thoughts somehow distinguishable from my own. It was more like a machine than an intelligence because there was no emotion (which usually is transmitted by humans). It was rapid and the rate of flow was constant. Telepathy from humans usually flows in waves. (At least this is how I perceive it.) It was much clearer and more intense than usual telepathy. The last message was received within a day or two of the UFO-boarding incident which occurred in Mississippi, only a few hundred miles from here. . . . I received the message before I knew of the UFO incident from TV. I have never seen a UFO except in pictures in magazines. I don't have hallucinations, nor have I received other messages (except occasional telepathy from humans). I have no desire to be famous. . . .

All four messages were exactly the same, and consist of:

1. A brief image of a flying saucer, a plain, grey, convex disk.
2. A sense of doubt.
3. A brief image of an ordinary clock face, hands blurred around the face.
4. A break in the message.

The symbols 2, 3, 2, 4 and 3 were then repeated and followed by a brief image of space with stars. . . .

Another man who has observed unusual objects in the sky on successive nights in early summer 1955 reports on some "interesting coincidences" involving dreams:

> The night after the second evening of sightings I had what I liked to think was a dream. . . . I was drawn up into the central object which I had observed. While inside I had a conversation with at least some of its occupants—people-like, not monsters. It was a conversation of "equals," that is I was not one of them. In essence I told them it was too soon. I wasn't ready to do the task I was supposed to, but that I would be ready at a set time to begin it, my thirty-second year, I believe, which if there is any truth to the dream should soon begin as I am now 32. In addition, I told them I wasn't able to handle the dreams and strange events that had been occurring, and that they should stop until I was able to handle them. . . .
>
> Prior to this "dream" I had a number of quasi-psychic events. I would frequently have dreams which while dreaming, I sensed were different from most dreams. And they invariably had a prophetic element. For instance, I would dream our house would catch fire, and the next day there was a fire in the kitchen, or once I woke up with a vivid image of the front page of the paper, and the morning newspaper was exactly that picture (the day they announced the Vanguard satellite program).

This letter is another indication that people with experiences similar to those of Uri Geller are not uncommon. It is possible to review and compare their impressions once a framework is created which permits them to come forward with their testimony without fear of ridicule.

Another correspondent, a woman with four children, relates an experience that involves a child and took place on November 28, 1972:

> At five o'clock in the morning this child awoke screaming, bringing his father into the room [note the parallel with the Dr. X case quoted in Chapter One]. He told his father that a blinding beam of light had shined on his arm pinning him to the bed! This was accompanied by a sound also. The hands of his electric clock on the wall were spinning madly. The boy said that all this going on at the same time frightened him.

When the mother questioned him later she was trying to establish the fact that it was a dream. The child stated in no uncertain terms that it was real and no dream. She tried to catch him again about the light "coming in through the window." He stated flatly that it came *right through the wall*. The mother said, "What made you so afraid?" whereupon the child replied: I thought it was robbers. But they said it was from Christ!

Additional comments have come to me from scientists in several countries. Professor Miklos, a Romanian researcher, offered a theory that may be helpful in our attempts to understand Uri Geller:

> In my view there may be—alternatively or in parallel— three main sources of psi phenomena: i) matter's evolutionary "ascent" gave birth, via brain-mind, to an apparently non-material entity. ii) there actually exists a non-material kind of "other world" which occasionally interacts with our material world. iii) there is the UFOs world that brings about psi-occurrences. . . .
>
> Just as there can be a matter-antimatter interaction there could also be a psi-nonpsi interaction; psi occurrences, or the part thereof we do observe and register, may represent surface processes (in analogy to surface

chemistry's interface phenomena) at the "boundary" sur-
faces of two or several worlds. This is somewhat related
to your interpenetrating universes. Your "metalogical"
preference is very close to my mind's heart. It is only
through metatheories that an established *Weltbild* can
be reiterated so that new observational-experimental
findings will be fitted in.

In later correspondence, Professor Miklos has added
that he is using the term "matter" as conceived by another
Romanian psychic researcher, Dr. V. Sakleanu, who postulates that matter has three aspects: substantial, energetical,
and informational. According to Miklos, in paranormal occurrences the last two aspects are manifesting themselves.
In this sense, "nonmaterial" should really be taken to
mean "nonsubstantial."

Among three possible psi sources identified by Miklos,
the simplest by its reference to currently accepted
theories, is the first one, because we can readily conceive
of the existence of an order of like form that would have
reached a higher evolutionary level than ours. Perhaps this
form of consciousness shares the planet with us, a fact that
would make it unnecessary to bring into our theories the
hypothesis of extraterrestrial visitors. Earlier in this book I
have speculated several times that UFO phenomena might
in fact originate on our own planet, and I think this hypothesis will deserve to be taken into consideration in any
future study.

We have reviewed much of the data on Geller that I felt
was relevant to the UFO problem, and I have tried to
show why I had been motivated to pursue this line of
research in spite of Geller's apparent unreliability. My
own observation of Geller was only one of the factors here;
the other was the convergence of his experience with
those of a sizable sample of individuals with whom I am in
contact. Now we must attempt to form a general picture of
all this. We must ask what the global nature of the phenomenon is. I propose the view that we are not dealing

with spontaneous manifestations that can be explained simply by the psychiatrist or by the student of ordinary spiritualist phenomena, such as automatic writing. Nor are we necessarily dealing with space visitors. We are dealing with a control system.

CHAPTER NINE

The Control System

Camilla: You, sir, should unmask.
Stranger: Indeed?
Cassilda: Indeed it's time. We have all
        laid aside disguise but you.
Stranger: I wear no mask.
Camilla: (*Terrified, aside to Cassilda*)
        No mask? No mask!

   —*The King in Yellow:* Act I, Scene 2
   by Robert W. Chambers

The Conditioning of *Homo Sapiens*

I think we are close, very close to understanding what
UFOs are, and what they do, although not necessarily how
they work, for in this area we still have much to observe
and learn before we can obtain the basis of a higher technology. But in order to grasp their nature and purpose we
have only to look around us and examine the shift that
takes place right now in human mythologies. To convince
ourselves of the reality of this change we need only observe to what extent the subject of extraterrestrial life has
become fashionable. We are as likely to find mention of it
today in the arguments of the scientists as in the statements of the fortune tellers. At one end of the academic
spectrum, modern radio astronomers suggest that we ought
to listen to the stars to decipher in the galactic noise the
possible murmur of newly born societies or the wise warn-

ings of long-disappeared cultures. At the popular end of the spectrum, Jeanne Dixon is quoted by a tabloid (which calls her "the best psychic in the U.S.") as prophesying an imminent change in our understanding of UFOs, "and it will bring great benefit to Mankind," she says.

According to an interview with Dixon published in May, 1974, the UFOs are flown by women pilots and come from a planet located beyond Jupiter, but still undiscovered: "The people in the UFOs are interested in us, but have avoided contacting us until now because we have not been mentally ready."

Ms. Dixon herself is a good example of the increasing number of people who are turning to a belief in UFO reality. We are, as a society, developing a great thirst for contact with superior minds that will provide guidance for our poor, harassed, hectic planet. In so doing we may be ready to fall into a trap, perhaps a kind, benevolent trap.

I believe that when we speak of UFO sightings as instances of space visitations we are looking at the phenomenon on the wrong level. We are not dealing with successive waves of visitations from space. We are dealing with a control system.

The thermostats that regulate your house temperature summer and winter constitute a control system, as I pointed out in the Introduction to this book. In summer, a thermostat allows the air to get warmer until a certain limit is reached, and then the cooling system is triggered. But in winter when the outside atmosphere turns cold, and temperature drops below another limit, then a different mechanism, the heater, comes into play and warms the house. A naïve observer might try to explain all this by assuming that warm is "good" and cold is "bad," and that certain moral laws apply. He would be right half the time. Another naïve observer of the opposite school might take a reversed view and decide that warm is "evil." He would succeed in explaining some of the behavior of the phenomenon (the cooling of the house) but not the whole. To understand the whole phenomenon one needs a grasp of the control concept, and one must be ready to understand that it needs two opposite principles for its function.

I propose the hypothesis that there is a control system for human consciousness. I have not determined whether it is natural or spontaneous; whether it is explainable in terms of genetics, of social psychology, or of ordinary phenomena—or if it is artificial in nature, and under the power of some superhuman will. It may be entirely determined by laws that we have not yet discovered.

I am led to this hypothesis by the fact that in every instance of the UFO phenomenon I have been able to study in depth I have found as many rational elements as I have absurd ones, and many that I could interpret as friendly and many that seemed hostile. No matter what approach I take, I can never explain more than half of the facts.

This is what tells me that I am working on the wrong level. And so do all the believers, and this definitely includes the skeptics, because they believe they can explain the facts as strongly as the most enthusiastic convert to Ms. Dixon's vision of Jupiterian Amazons! I would argue that they are all wrong, even Puharich with his disappearing tapes, and Uri voicing from Rhombus 4-D.

There are ways to gain access to the reference level of every control system I know. Even a child, if smart or daring enough, can climb on a chair, change the dial of a thermostat and elicit a response. (The response in question might be a sound spanking from his father, of course. The road to higher knowledge has such accidents.) It must be possible to gain access to the control of the UFO phenomenon, to forget the spirits and the pranks of Rhombus 4-D, and do some real science. But it will take a very smart approach—or a very daring one.

The Schedule of Reinforcement

Consider the graph of Figure 3. It shows the development of the UFO waves between 1947 and 1962. I have not extended it to the present because there is too much work here for one man. To obtain such a graph one has to collect all available sightings and examine them one at a time for possible rejection causes. Then one needs to classify them as to type and reliability, assigning a weight to each selected case and aggregating these weights to obtain a monthly index of UFO activity. Finally, one needs to eliminate the trend, the background variation, from fluctuations of the curve, in order to extract the cyclic variations.

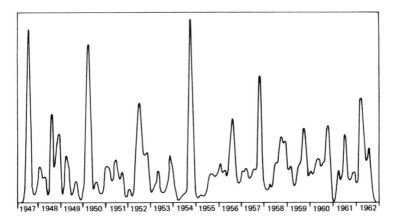

1947 1948 1949 1950 1951 1952 1953 1954 1955 1956 1957 1958 1959 1960 1961 1962

Figure 3. The pattern of UFO activity (trend removed) between 1947 and 1962. Is this a schedule of reinforcement?

Figure 3 shows the variations of an external phenomenon (the UFO manifestations) to which human society is reacting in various ways. It is interesting to ask whether this process is not subtly changing us.

The controversial work of psychologist B. F. Skinner has shown under what conditions an organism reacting to an external phenomenon *learns* a new behavior. We also know under what conditions this learning is irreversible. These are similar to the pattern that the UFO phenomenon seems to be following. Is it trying to teach us something? With every new wave of UFOs, the social impact becomes greater. More young people become fascinated with space, with psychic phenomena, with new frontiers in consciousness. More books and articles appear, changing our culture in the direction of a higher image of man.

Skinner has been working for half a century to study behavior and the process of modifying it. His experiments, which are hotly debated by his colleagues, have centered on observations of rats, pigeons, and other animals placed in reinforcement situations. I am indebted to Mr. Fred Beckman of the University of Chicago and to Professor Price-Williams of UCLA for the suggestion that these researches might have a bearing on a discussion of human reactions to UFOs.

> The technological use of schedules of reinforcement is rapidly expanding. . . . Techniques involving schedules have been adapted to a wide range of species. Surprisingly similar performances, particularly under complex schedules, have been demonstrated in organisms as diverse as the pigeon, mouse, rat, dog, cat and monkey. At the human level the analysis of schedules has proved useful in the study of psychotic behavior and in the design of educational techniques for normal human subjects. . . . Other applications to the problem of the control of human behavior, as in law and penology, religion, industry, and commerce, offer considerable promise.

The above appears in a highly technical volume called *Patterns of Reinforcement* by Ferster and B. F. Skinner (Appleton-Century, 1957) reporting on research sponsored by the Office of Naval Research.

Although the design of their experiments is complex, the findings of Ferster and Skinner can be summarized in a few lines. Drastic modification of the behavior of an animal (including man) can be achieved by selectively reinforcing certain actions (for instance by giving food to a pigeon only when he presses a certain lever). However, certain ways of reinforcing behavior lead to better learning than others. If the training is too even and monotonous the subject may stop in its development, or even return to an earlier state; *the best schedule of reinforcement is one that combines periodicity with unpredictability.* Learning is then slow but continuous. It leads to the highest level of adaptation. And it is irreversible. *It is interesting to ask whether the pattern of UFO waves does not have the same effect as a schedule of reinforcement.*

A newspaper column commented upon the apparent lack of reality of the whole UFO phenomenon: "It does not attack us. It does not affect our daily lives. It does not help us with our many problems. It has brought us nothing of value. It may have scared a few folks here and there, but then so do thunder storms and tornadoes. The whole thing, as a social issue, is of no consequence whatsoever." The journalist who wrote this column was superficially right, of course. But he forgot another fact: human life is not ruled by the juxtaposition of problem-solving exercises. Human life is ruled by imagination and myth; these obey strict laws and they, too, are governed by control systems, although admittedly not of the hardware type. *If UFOs are having an action at that level it will be almost impossible to detect it by conventional methods.*

If UFO activity operates in a fashion similar to Skinner's reinforcement, which is the least amenable to extinction (although it is slow and steady), then the learning will take time but it will never be forgotten.

How can we verify whether such conditioning is in fact operating?

We should firmly establish the primary effects. We should go on analyzing landing traces, punching IBM cards, and scrutinizing the heavens with cameras and radio telescopes, but this activity will be completely useless if it is not related to an investigation of the secondary impact, the shift in our world-view that the phenomenon produces. A phenomenon that denies itself, that annihilates evidence of itself cannot be mastered by engineering brute force. If the logic of the UFO phenomenon is a meta-logic, it is not useful to gather in the evenings around a spoon Uri Geller has bent, and to wait in the dark for cosmic messages. More kitchen utensils will become useless, and there will be cosmic messages, to be sure! But any expectations of higher wisdom will be soon brought to nought by their insane incoherence or their calculated fallacy, even if they are couched in the higher language of tensor calculus.

If the phenomenon is forcing us through a learning curve then it MUST mislead us. When Skinner designs a machine that feeds a rat only when the right lever is depressed, this is extremely misleading for the rat! But if the rat doesn't do it he becomes extremely hungry. Man is hungry for knowledge and power, and if there is an intelligence behind the UFOs it must have taken this fact into account. We also tend to forget that we have no choice. We *must* eventually study UFOs.

A civilization such as ours, which is entirely oriented toward what it regards as technical progress, cannot afford long to ignore the apparition in the sky of objects that defy the laws of its physics and the performance of its rocket planes. Within a few years the advanced countries will place on this problem, openly or in secret, their best physicists, their best intelligence specialists, their best computer scientists. But they may be powerless to utilize their expertise, because the phenomenon fits none of these categories. If this is so, then UFOs can never be analyzed or conceived, because *they are the means through which man's concepts are being rearranged.* All we can do is to trace their effects on humans.

We have seen that the control system operates like a thermostat. It progresses by oscillations, drawing from the antagonism of fire and ice, warm and cold, evil and good, all myths for the feeble minds of men, equally bound by higher laws. For hot and cold are only relative to a mean, two appearances of a single fact, the motion of molecules. Few people have grasped both the physics and the beauty of it.

What is the variable being controlled in this control system? Thermostats control temperature; gyroscopes control the direction in which a rocket flies. What could a paranormal phenomenon control? *I suggest that it is human belief that is being controlled and conditioned.*

The Level of Control

Like the Stranger in *The King in Yellow*, the UFO wears no mask. It is exactly what we see, but to understand it we must face it squarely.

My assumption is that a level of control of society exists which is a regulator of man's development. I am also led to the assumption that the action of UFOs operates at this level. What does this explain? *First it explains why there is no contact.* Direct genuine contact would ruin the experiment. (There may be deliberately *misleading* contact, as in UMMO.) It would preclude genuine learning. It explains some of the statements made by ufonauts ("you should believe in us but not too much"), and the Schirmer case, with its deliberate confusion: "you will not speak wisely about this night." It explains the absurdity of many cases, where reactions to the phenomenon may have been evoked in terms of nonverbal consciousness rather than in "logical" terms. This would explain why so many witnesses are incapable of finding words to describe what they have seen.

When I speak of a control system for planet earth I do not want my words to be misunderstood: I do not mean that some higher order of beings has locked us inside the constraints of a space-bound jail, closely monitored by psychic entities we might call angels or demons. I do not propose to redefine God. What I do mean is that mythology rules at a level of our social reality over which normal political and intellectual action has no real power. At that level, time frames are long, of the order of a century, and evolution is slow and sure. Mass media, which are designed to give split-second images of transient noise (the noisier the better), miss this signal entirely. A society with an attention span of ten minutes (the interval between two TV commercials) can have no concept of events that have begun when my grandfather was not yet born and will end after my grandson dies. But there *are* such long-term changes and they may be deliberate. They dominate the destiny of civilizations. Myths define the set of things scholars, politicians, and scientists can think about. They are operated upon by symbols, and the language these symbols form constitutes a complete system. This system is meta-logical, but not metaphysical. It violates no laws because it is the substance of which laws are made.

The theory does not explain how UFOs are made to appear to us although it gives support to one idea about them: that they are constructed *both as physical craft* (a fact which has long appeared to me undeniable) *and as psychic devices,* whose exact properties remain to be defined. As a focus for psychic phenomena, the UFO evokes a deep emotional reaction in the viewer, but logical development of an investigation is prevented—or precluded— by the apparent violations of causality that surround it and by the sociological climate that is created. Scientists may be willing to interview a witness who has seen a landed craft, but he may not wish to talk to them. Or the witness may offer as "proof" of his experience a couple of pancakes given to him by extraterrestrials, a recitation of meaningless messages, or a story of sexual contact with a girl from outer space. In any case, a pursuit of the rational study of the case is impossible. The lurid aspects of many such stories make their serious examination improbable, and this in turn reinforces the role of the UFO rumors as folklore, rich in new images.

The Next Form of Religion

In the course of ten years of investigation into paranormal phenomena one hears many stories. In the past, I have only published those stories I could authenticate or that I feel meet basic criteria of reliability. Beyond these cases, however, I have been exposed to a certain number of consistent rumors which do play a role in the unfolding of the total myth. They involved stories of contact between humans and alleged visitors residing on earth. Some of the descriptions are extremely detailed and have involved scientists as witnesses. Some of the humans associated with the cases are said to have eventually disappeared. There is a spectrum of experience that runs from abduction or contact (conscious or not), to the close-encounter, to the exposure to humanoids, and, finally, to the reports of aliens among us. I have spent hours with Betty and Barney Hill and have had a chance to discuss the case of their abduction with Dr. Simon. I have also become acquainted with the stories of people who exhibited paranormal faculties and claimed to derive them from sources in outer space.

What interests me is not the likelihood of such a contact (how could we prove it?) but the fact that a subculture now exists in every country, based on the idea that humanity has a higher destiny. You will find people in remote towns of California who have literally dropped out of city life (where they had held responsible positions and enjoyed good salaries) because they had received messages from space instructing them to do so. These people are not hippies, although similar experiences have been frequent also among younger commune members. The people I am referring to are middle-aged, have families and steady jobs. They would be regarded as perfectly square if it were not for the fact that their lives have been changed by what they consider to be genuine extraterrestrial communication. They wait. And, a curious fact in the current state of the world, they seem perfectly happy. We could categorize them among the victims of city pressures who have sought the psychological comfort of small-town life. But we might also wonder whether they are not the forerunners of a new spiritual movement.

One such man left Los Angeles with his family after a message he believes came from Jupiter instructed him to find an isolated spot and live in semiretirement, "providing a center of peace in the world of intense turmoil that was to come." He now lives with his wife in a small mountain village, has no television set, reads avidly, and awaits further instructions. He is one of the happiest old people I have met in the United States. We are not here dealing with escapism—we are dealing with the next form of religion.

Why bring all this into the open? Because flying saucers, real or not as objects, clearly introduce a central element in an already troubled future landscape. It would be overly optimistic to predict that they will decrease its dangers. It is nonetheless interesting to ask what will happen to our civilization if the next step in the development of the phenomenon is a massive change of human attitudes toward paranormal abilities and extraterrestrial life. While many conservative scientists still refuse even to consider the data, and while many gullible people have already jumped to blind belief in some occult mumbo-jumbo, it seems important to me that an increasing number of scientists continue to promote the exploration of new concepts by seriously studying the phenomena.

A great celebration, in San Francisco. A thousand young people, the nucleus of everything psychic and counter-cultural in Northern California, have gathered in a large auditorium. There are booths selling health food, cosmic advice, tantric yoga courses, and consciousness training. A colorful crowd pulsates through the aisles and fills the seminar rooms. The One World Family Commune of Berkeley runs a restaurant. It is directed by Allan the Messiah, wearing an impeccable red uniform and advertising the Everlasting Gospel revealed to him by the saucers. His information indicates that the earth is in fact hollow, with the saucer people inside.

"Do you really believe that?" asks a friend of mine.

"Certainly," he replies. "If you were going to make a planet, would you waste all that good dirt?"

I find myself on a panel with Andrija Puharich, Arthur Young, mathematician Charles Muses (Young and Muses are the two authors of an excellent book called *Consciousness and Reality*) and a scientist, Tom Bearden. The panel is chaired by Ira Einhorn, a poet from Philadelphia. Puharich describes his latest experiences with Geller. He explains to the audience that he gets messages on his tape recorder, coming from a mysterious cosmic source. But the tape vanishes regularly. There is nothing he can do to prevent it, and he is totally committed to the idea that he and Uri are now guided by a very high source of wisdom, and that the only course for mankind is to place its destiny in "their" hands.

Ira gives the floor to Charles Muses who comments on Geller. Humanity, he says, stands on the brink of catastrophe, at the edge of a chasm. How are we to reach the safe side? A flying saucer hovers above the chasm, our only hope: "Do you want a lift?" asks the UFO.

Salvation from heaven. Shouldn't we know something more about the helpful stranger before we jump on board? Shouldn't we make sure that the chasm is real, and that we cannot bridge it with our own resources? Cannot we reach the other side by our own means?

When we are asked to suspend all our rational thoughts, to forget our "obsolete" critical faculties, to throw control overboard, then the time has come to take all the data and go away with it to a quiet place to think. My guess is that the problem will not be seriously studied by many scientists until it has begun to generate a very high degree of public awareness, and then the approach will be an entirely classical one: millions of dollars to consultants and research institutes, thousands of questionnaires, field investigators with glass bottles, sociologists filling correlation matrices, medical personnel adjusting electrodes over the frontal lobes of ranchers. But this will only be, in my opinion, *another wrinkle in the learning curve, another step in the conditioning.*

There is a strange urge in my mind: I would like to stop behaving as a rat pressing levers—even if I have to go hungry for a while. I would like to step outside the conditioning maze and see what makes it tick. I wonder what I would find. Perhaps a terrible superhuman monstrosity the very contemplation of which would make a man insane? Perhaps a solemn gathering of wise men? Or the maddening simplicity of unattended clockwork?

Conclusion

Time and again in the history of civilizations, there arises some wonderful untruth around which magnificent energy crystallizes, and great deeds are done. Such a time has come again. *It has become very important for large numbers of people to expect visitors from outer space.*

As I was discussing Uri Geller's abilities with British scholar Gordon Creighton, driving through the midst of London in the winter of 1973—a winter plagued by strikes and the energy crisis—Creighton gave me a definition of myth that clarified the confusion of many approaches to the contemporary problems of UFOs. "People mistakenly believe, he said, that a myth is an untruth. But myth is not that. A myth is that which is TRUER THAN TRUTH."

It may not be true that flying saucers represent visits from outer space. But if large enough numbers believe it, then in some sense it will become *truer than true*, long enough for certain things to change irreversibly.

Some of the best informed sources of gossip in Washington are convinced that UFOs will be increasingly prominent in coming years. There are persistent rumors highly placed officials in the U.S. government have long had evidence that another form of intelligence was contacting us. The stage is set for another UMMO. A former aerospace engineer turned UFO lecturer even believes that at the occasion of the Bicentennial the government will announce that there is life on Mars, and that a meeting between U.S. representatives and extraterrestrials is imminent!

These people are going down an interesting path, one that Puharich has already traveled with enthusiasm. He predicts a mass landing. Ten years ago such statements would not have been taken seriously. But today they are eagerly listened to, evoking fear or passion in their audiences; tomorrow some higher officials may join the ranks of the believers. The UMMO affair, the case of AFFA, and the predictions of Mrs. Keech (of *When Prophecy Fails*) have involved sincere people, holding responsible positions. Slowly a climate has been created in which a much larger number now participate in the myth-making. The belief is reinforced by successive waves of sightings. Skepticism is eroded. The cases are giving more and more evidence of the reality of the UFOs—but this evidence is so constructed as to elude classical analysis by scientists. Perhaps the UFOs are not behaving according to our laws of causality. Perhaps their time flows differently from ours. Perhaps their logic is a meta-logic.

The observable change is an increasing willingness to believe in extraterrestrial life. Attitudes on this subject among scientists, the media, and the public have indeed totally changed in twenty years. We can rationalize this change; we can attribute it solely to the progress of radio astronomy and the pioneering work of a few biologists. Or we can recognize it for what it is—*the result of a shifting of our mythological structure, the human learning curve bending toward a new cosmic behavior. When this irreversible learning is achieved, the UFO phenomenon may go away entirely. Or it may assume some suitable representation on a human scale. The angels may land downtown.*

For a long time I have harbored the private belief that the organizations responsible for our collective security were secretly conducting a large-scale, quiet, and competent investigation into the nature of the paranormal phenomena that are manifested around us. If I still believed it today I would not be publishing this book.

When I saw the blunders of Project Blue Book and its biased conclusions I imagined that the project was only a front to keep civilian scientists from poking their inquisitive noses into a very serious matter that was regarded in high places as an important item. When I noticed that certain files had disappeared from the Blue Book archives and that the best photographic evidence was missing, I rationalized my disappointment into the reassuring thought that somebody, somewhere, was gathering this evidence and studying it in earnest. When I saw that Air Force bases around the world were sending to government organizations copies of all their information on UFOs, I saw this as a confirmation of the coverup theory—and I did not think it was my role, as an inexperienced scientist, to challenge it. Today I am no longer young, and I have lost my unquestioning trust of official wisdom in matters of advanced research.

In recent years, thanks to several members of the Invisible College, and thanks to other friends in Europe, I have had a chance to examine many documents like the ones I have quoted. Far from revealing government authorities engaged in quiet research, they give a picture of incoherent restlessness in every country. Meeting behind closed doors, scientists and military men swap scary stories, while the real phenomena go on, unstudied, unconcerned, UNIDENTIFIED!

For a long time I have believed that science would gradually realize the importance of paranormal phenomena as an opportunity to expand its theories of the world. I thought that here was our only chance to redefine human dignity in the world to come.

I now believe differently.

It is not simply our freedom that is in danger now. It is a certain concept of humanity. And it is no longer to science that we must turn to understand the nature of this psychic crisis and find its key. Nor will the answer be discovered in some secret file in Washington. The solution lies where it has always been: *within ourselves*. We can reach it any time we want.

Bibliography

For additional details and references concerning the UFO controversy the reader could consult the following sources.

Blum, R. and J. *Beyond Earth*. New York: Bantam, 1974.
Fuller, J. *Incident at Exeter*. New York: Putnam, 1967.
Hynek, J. A. *The UFO Experience*. Chicago: Regnery, 1973.
Hynek, J. A. and Vallee, J. *The Edge of Reality*. Chicago: Regnery, 1975.
Jung, C. G. *Flying Saucers: A Modern Myth of Things Seen in the Skies*. New York: Harcourt Brace, 1959.
Michel, A. *Flying Saucers and the Straight-Line Mystery*. New York: Criterion, 1958.
Ruppelt, E. J. *The Report on UFOs*. New York: Ace Books, 1956.

Flying Saucer Review (bimonthly), published by FSR Publications, Ltd. 281 Camden High St., London NW1, England.

Index